D1616000

IN RUSSIAN WONDERLAND

AN AMERICAN'S ODYSSEY

IN SOVIET RUSSIA

CHARLES COLE

Print ISBN: 978-0-9996032-0-8

Ebook ISBN: 978-0-9996032-1-5

First U.S. Edition

Cole, Charles

This book is dedicated to the memory of those Russian teachers of the Defense Language Institute who not only taught me the Russian language over 50 years ago, but also gave their students a basic understanding of the Soviet Union without which this book could not have been written.

CONTENTS

PREFACE

When I get home, I shall write a book about this place.
If I . . . If I ever *do* get home.
—from Disney's 1951 film adaptation
of Lewis Carroll's *Alice in Wonderland*

Friends have asked why I chose to write this book. There are several answers on various levels, which I shall discuss below. But first, a few words as to my background.

As a young boy in ninth grade in 1960, I developed an interest in foreign languages with my study of Latin. My classmates were neither interested in studying Latin, nor were they particularly adept at it. I, on the other hand, seemed to have a natural talent for learning new vocabulary and applying grammar rules. For me, it was actually fun.

I continued my study of Latin throughout high school, adding two years of French along the way. After an unsuccessful freshman year in college, it became clear that I was not at all ready for the experience. So, I joined the US Army and was assigned to study Russian at a highly unique school—the Defense Language Institute (DLI) in Monterey, California. Following over a year and a half of intense study at DLI (six hours daily, five days each week), I was assigned to the Army Security Agency.

After a brief course in using Russian in military communications intelligence missions, I was deployed to a small border-listening post in West Germany, where I served until my discharge in 1969. We monitored Soviet military radio communications as part of America's "early warning" system of military preparedness.

Four years of military service had a very positive effect on my maturity and readiness to undertake serious academic study. Since I had a solid foundation in Russian by this time, upon returning to college I decided to major in Russian and German and graduated in just over two years. Shortly before my graduation in 1972, one of my college professors informed me that a US government cultural exchange exhibit was going to the Soviet Union.[1]

My professor strongly encouraged me to apply for this program. He felt it would be a wonderful opportunity to enhance my knowledge of and ability to actively use Russian. He was right. This six-month tour of duty inside the Soviet Union provided me with a total immersion environment from which I was well prepared to benefit, thanks to having studied and worked with the Russian language for six years prior to this trip. It also gave me a chance to view the world in which we lived at that time from a truly unique perspective.

That brings me to the rationale for writing this book. First, aside from the linguistic benefits described above, this assignment also gave me a chance to see for myself what the Soviet Union and Communism were all about. I only wish that more people of my generation had been able to witness what I did in the USSR in 1972. Forty-five years later, I would like to share my experiences with my fellow Americans of all ages.

Much can be learned by examining history. I hope that today's generation can learn from the information that was shared with me by my old Russian teachers at DLI in the 1960s, from my subsequent study of Soviet and Russian history, and from my firsthand observations of a totalitarian socialist society. As British philosopher George Santayana noted long ago, "Those that fail to learn from history are doomed to repeat it."

Second, a comprehensive review of relevant literature reveals that no one who served as a "guide" on a USIA (United States Information Agency) cultural exchange exhibit in the Soviet Union seems to have written in detail about their experiences of

---

1. Details of this program are discussed in the Introduction.

having told America's story to Soviet citizens in their language and in their country. Thus, this book is unique in that way.

Third, given the amount of attention being paid to Russia these days, I believe a glimpse of the society that produced today's Russian Federation will help provide information necessary to better understand that society. This book should help the reader do that.

Finally, I was shocked by a sight on an evening news show wrapping up the presidential election coverage in 2012. A group of young people had assembled outside the fence surrounding the White House to celebrate the election results. They enthusiastically chanted over and over: "Karl Marx, Karl Marx. Socialism, Socialism." I was genuinely taken aback by this and wondered whether they could be serious, given the documented historical record of life under socialism in virtually every country in which it has been implemented.

More recently, in the primary election campaign of 2016, large numbers of young Americans actively supported a self-proclaimed socialist candidate for the presidency. I was again astounded at how uninformed these young folks seemed to be as to what history teaches us about what can happen when a large centralized government wields unchecked power over people.

It is axiomatic that young people are optimistic and idealistic. Sir Winston Churchill is reported to have noted that if one is not a socialist by age eighteen, he has no heart. How easy it is in youth to heed the siren call of a seductive ideology—one that, tragically, has been responsible for the murder of many millions of innocent people over the centuries.

I have heard it said that "such things can never happen here." I'm sure many Russians felt that way a hundred years ago. However, I vividly recall the heartfelt stories told to me over fifty years ago by several of my DLI Russian teachers, many of whom were in their sixties. They recounted how, as youngsters around the time of the Russian Revolution, they sat at the dinner table listening to their parents and grandparents lament what was happening to their beloved Russia.

The saddest part is that these people were absolutely

powerless to stop the riotous anarchy enveloping their nation. The fortunate ones escaped to the West. The less fortunate were treated to revolution, civil war, Lenin's terror, not to mention Stalin's famine, purges, and slave labor camps—the GULAG. Tragically, many met their end by Stalin's firing squads.

It is of these things I first learned at DLI during my eighteen-month study of Russian and later during my college experience. Then came my journey through "Wonderland"[2] in 1972. It was in that far-off place that I witnessed events eerily similar to things I'm starting to see in my own country today. I hope that, after joining me in my odyssey, readers of this book will make similar mental associations and relate them to current events as I have. It's almost as if I'm watching a movie, the ending of which I've already seen. And it's not a pretty picture at all.

As author and scholar Thomas Sowell has noted, "We cannot return to the past, even if we wanted to, but let us hope that we can learn something from the past to make for a better present and future." I invite readers to join me on my 1972 journey, in the hope that we can all learn something from it that might help us better understand the trials and tribulations the Russian people endured on their difficult and still incomplete journey to freedom and self-governance.

Charles E. Cole
2017

---

2. Many former Soviet citizens who escaped from the USSR used the Russian term *strana chudes* when referring to the Soviet Union. That is the Russian equivalent for "wonderland," as in the Lewis Carroll work *Alice in Wonderland.* It is a derisive term these people employed to describe their Kafkaesque life in the USSR.

FOREWORD

The times and events described in this book occurred in 1972 in what was then known as the Union of Soviet Socialist Republics (USSR)—or the Soviet Union.

The USSR ceased to exist as a government in December of 1991. Thus, it is quite likely that people under the age of thirty-five don't remember the Soviet Union at all. They, along with many other Americans, most probably remember only the brief attention the USSR typically received in high school history textbooks.

Even though the Soviet Union has been replaced by today's Russia, knowing something about it is important to understand the country now known as the Russian Federation. To set the context for the reader, a short historical background on the Soviet Union is thus in order.

Russia as a country dates back to the ninth century, when it was called *Rus*. Its first tsar was Ivan the Terrible in the sixteenth century, and in 1721, Russia was officially established as an empire by Tsar Peter the Great, who ruled from 1682 until his death in 1725. He was of the lineage referred to as the Romanov Dynasty, which ruled Russia for just over three hundred years until its last tsar, Nicholas II, abdicated the throne in March of 1917. Later that year, the Bolshevik wing of the Communist Party staged a successful revolution and took control of the country, proclaiming it a Socialist state under the leadership of Vladimir Lenin.[1]

---

1. The other wing of the Russian Communist Party was known as the Mensheviks—or the "minority" wing of the Party. They were more cerebral Marxists, whereas the Bolsheviks represented the "revolution now" radical wing dedicated to the immediate overthrow of the tsarist monarchy at any cost.

A civil war ensued pitting the "Reds" (i.e., the Communists) against the "White Guard," a confederation of anti-Communists and monarchists. This ended in the early 1920s, and the victorious Reds consolidated all power in the Communist Party, which dominated the Soviet Government for almost seventy years thereafter.

Lenin is considered the founder of the old Soviet Union, and he was the undisputed ruler of the Communist Party until his death in 1924. He was the first of the Communist leaders to employ terror as a means of controlling society. Later in that decade, the infamous dictator Josef Stalin became the absolute ruler of the Communist Party and the Soviet Government and remained so until his death in 1953.

Stalin's rule in Soviet Russia was characterized by a host of calamities for the Russian people—forced collectivization of all agriculture, resulting famines, and purges of party and military leaders, which included show trials, executions, and deportation of "enemies of the people" to the infamous GULAG, a network of hundreds of slave labor camps extending from the Urals to the far reaches of eastern Siberia. Millions of mostly innocent people perished in these camps.

A major event for the Russian people was the invasion by Hitler's armies in 1941. In the USSR, this four-year war (known in the West as World War II) was called the "Great Patriotic War." Over twenty-five million Soviets perished in this conflict—one in which virtually every family in the Soviet Union of that time lost someone.

During the postwar years, Stalin forcibly imposed Communist rule throughout the Eastern European countries that the Red Army had "liberated" from the Germans, as well as in the Baltic States—Estonia, Latvia, and Lithuania. The latter were reabsorbed into the Soviet Union, and the Eastern European countries became puppet regimes—totally subservient to Moscow.

The period from 1946 to 1991 was called the "Cold War." It pitted the United States and its allies in Western Europe and Asia against the Soviet Union and its satellite countries of Eastern

Europe, as well as Communist China. In 1949, the Soviets detonated an atomic bomb, and the specter of a nuclear war raised the stakes in this geopolitical confrontation considerably.

After Stalin's death in 1953, a series of Soviet leaders emerged and ruled the country with an iron fist throughout the 1950s, '60s, '70s, and early '80s.[2] These years were noted for scarcity of consumer goods, an arms race with the United States, governmental corruption, and total domination of every aspect of Soviet life by the ruling Communist Party. Tight control of the country was ensured by the Soviet military and by the infamous secret police—the KGB. The country's borders were tightly sealed, and escape from this huge prison camp of a country was virtually impossible.

Three well-known instances of Soviet enforcement of control over their satellites occurred when Soviet tanks were sent to squelch popular uprisings in East Germany (1953), Hungary (1956), and Czechoslovakia (1968). The Soviet Union of that era, including the Brezhnev era during which my trip to the USSR took place, was characterized by total domination over the population of the Soviet Union and its satellite nations.

This all began to change in the mid-1980s with the leadership of Mikhail Gorbachev, who took power in 1985 and held it through the years of *perestroika* (rebuilding) and *glasnost* (openness).[3] Strict Soviet control of its Eastern European satellites was relaxed, leading to radical changes in those countries in the late 1980s (East Germany, Hungary, Czechoslovakia, Poland, and Romania). This, in turn, resulted in these countries renouncing Communism and in 1989–90 becoming independent, democratic states. The same then occurred in the Baltic states of Estonia, Latvia, and Lithuania

---

2. These included Nikita Khrushchev (1954–64), Leonid Brezhnev (1964–82), Yuri Andropov (1982–84), and Konstantin Chernenko (1984–85).

3. For Russian linguists reading this book, you will note that the palatalizing at the end of certain words in this text do not carry the traditional transliteration symbol ('). Thus, words such as *Rus, tsar, glasnost,* and Kazan appear under their traditional English spelling (i.e., without reference to the word final palatalization of the Russian consonant).

in 1990–91 when these former Soviet "republics" declared their independence from Moscow.

The Soviets were clearly no longer willing or able to enforce "Socialist unity" with tanks. Gorbachev became the first (and last) President of the Soviet Union in 1990, and he left office in December of 1991 when the Soviet Government collapsed and the USSR broke up into fifteen independent countries—one of which is today's Russian Federation.

Again, the focus of this book is on the Brezhnev era of the early 1970s—a time when every facet of Soviet life was rigidly controlled and dissent was swiftly and often brutally put down. This context is important to keep in mind as the reader progresses through the book.[4]

This stone figure of an oppressed human being was photographed in one of the Baltic States in 1972. Although it was erected as a tribute to the suffering of the people during World War II, it could have just as easily represented the daily agony endured by people throughout the USSR for almost seventy years.

---

4. A more detailed history of the Soviet Union is available from the sources listed in the selected bibliography at the end of this book.

Regimentation and total subservience to the regime were the order of the day in the USSR.

INTRODUCTION

Own only what you can always carry with you:
know languages, know countries, know people.
Let your memory be your travel bag.
—Russian writer Aleksandr Solzhenitsyn

From 1959 to 1991, the United States Information Agency (USIA) managed to reach millions of Soviet citizens through a series of cultural exchange exhibitions. Over the years, more than twenty such exhibits toured the old USSR. They employed Russian-speaking guides who brought the exhibits to life through their personal interactions with the millions of Soviet citizens who attended these events in the numerous cities in which they were held. The USIA divided these one-year cultural exchange exhibits to the USSR into six-month tours of duty.

This program was indeed unique. Several of the places the Soviets allowed the exhibits to be shown had previously been "closed" cities, meaning they had been totally off-limits to all foreigners. The residents of those cities had never met an American, and this program brought them face to face with several young Americans—Russian-speaking guides, as we were called.

The exhibits were part of an exchange program whereby the Soviets got something they wanted—mostly the ability to send some of their brightest students to American universities for advanced studies, primarily, I was told, in the hard sciences. In exchange for that, the Soviet Government allowed the USIA to send in groups of Russian-speaking young men and women who served as guides at the exhibits. This permitted us to interact directly with Soviet citizens in their native language—a benefit one USIA professional told me was worth its weight in gold.

There were other avenues of getting information through the Iron Curtain, such as *Radio Free Europe, Radio Liberty,* and *Voice of America* broadcasts in Russian. But these were heavily jammed by the Soviets and were very difficult to hear over a small Soviet-made radio. Also, any Soviet citizen caught listening to these "prohibited broadcasts" was subject to harassment by the KGB—the Soviet secret police—and harsh punishment, including incarceration.

To understand the importance of the exhibit program, one must keep in mind that the Soviet Union was a totally closed society ruled from the top by a small group of Communists: the Politburo of the Central Committee of the Communist Party of the USSR. The Communist Party was the only permitted political party, and the organs of the press and broadcast media were totally under its control. So was the dissemination of all information.

Since the days of Vladimir Lenin—the founder of the Soviet Union—the only information available to the Soviet people had been totally controlled by the government. Censorship was ironclad and virtually impenetrable. People deprived of factual news stories and taught one and only one political ideology (Marxism-Leninism) from their earliest years were easier to control than their counterparts in the West who had a broad array of information sources. There was no rule of law in the Soviet Union to protect basic civic and civil rights such as freedom of speech, freedom of the press, religious freedom, the right to bear arms, and the right of free assembly, to mention but a few such rights people enjoy in most western societies.

Soviet citizens had none of these rights. In fact, they had to register with the local police and had to show identity cards, including a *propiska*—their registration card—to any Soviet authority at any time. This severely limited their right to move about inside their own country.

Given this environment, imagine how exciting it was for Soviet visitors to an American cultural exchange exhibit to be able to dialogue with Russian-speaking Americans. For many, it was the experience of a lifetime, and they wanted to know everything about the USA. Their questions ranged from economics to daily life in America, to how one obtained this mysterious thing called "credit" in order to make a purchase, and even (and most interestingly) to politics.

Visitors to American exhibits during the Cold War seemed eager for information about life in the United States, and while many of the questions we would encounter had to do with the objects on display at the exhibit, the conversations would always include many, many inquiries about our daily lives as Americans. This was something they would never be able to ascertain from the one-sided propaganda that inundated them in their media.

Quite predictably, whenever visitors began asking political questions, there always seemed to be someone in the audience who would interrupt and say, "Young man, tell me about that gadget there," pointing to an exhibit item on display. This was a dog whistle for the Soviet visitors that meant "Stop asking political questions—we don't want those things discussed and we *are* watching and listening." Quite often, many of the Soviets around that part of the exhibit would get the message and silently walk away.

But, as will be shown in the subsequent chapters of this book, there were priceless moments when it was very clear that the message we were conveying was getting through and that previously "prohibited" thoughts or ideas managed to penetrate the ideological firewall. At times, average Soviet citizens would speak up and indirectly defend our positions.

I recall one elderly woman saying to me, "So, tell me about this matter of multiple political parties in your country." She was having trouble understanding why in the world a country would need two political parties. After all, as she said, the Communist Party of the Soviet Union took care of people's every need, from healthcare to education, to employment, to defending them from foreign enemies, to providing services for the elderly, etc.

I tried valiantly to explain to her the concept of a competition of ideas in which two rival political parties made differing cases to the public on matters of public policy. We talked for about ten minutes, at the end of which she said, "That's chaos," and walked away, shaking her head. She was totally incapable of understanding the core idea behind a genuine democracy. Not surprising since she had been exposed to only one ideology and one view of governance her entire life. Now she had come in contact with an alternate world view for which she was not prepared. But perhaps this conversation got her thinking. We always hoped it would.

There were also moments when our efforts clearly produced fruit. One makes me smile to this day. We were in the Soviet Union in 1972—an American election year. Several guides were supporters of Richard Nixon's reelection, but there were some who preferred Senator George McGovern. After a long day at the exhibit, I was leaving the pavilion to return to our hotel when I overheard two young Russian men talking about an amazing thing that they had witnessed. Seems they had walked around the entire exhibit asking the guides which candidate they supported in the election. They could not believe the disparity in the answers they got. One guide would say, "I'm for President Nixon because he's more qualified than McGovern." Another would say, "I'm for McGovern because I don't like Nixon's policies." One apparently even said, "I'm definitely voting for McGovern, because Nixon is a *svoloch'*."[1]

The very idea that an American government employee (which we were) would call the leader of his country an S.O.B. in public, in the Soviet Union, and in front of a Soviet audience during the Cold War simply boggled their minds. One can explain freedom of speech all day long, but a single real-life example such as this sows the seeds for serious contemplation by people who have never encountered such a phenomenon. As an old Russian proverb puts it, "Better to see something once than to hear about it a hundred times."

Each annual exhibit had a theme. Ours was "Research and Development in the USA." We had on display a wide variety

---

1. The Russian word *svoloch'* translates to S.O.B.

of products that had been produced by American companies as a result of commercial research and development. We even had the actual command module of the Apollo 10 spacecraft posted just outside the entrance to the exhibit hall. The other items ranged from small kitchen gadgets to three American-made automobiles to a then-state-of-the-art Univac computer. These were things that average Soviet citizens of that era could only dream of.[2] They were amazed at the array of exhibited items, and this, too, left an indelible imprint on many visitors' minds, as they now had something tangible by which to evaluate the daily Soviet propaganda that portrayed the United States as a backward, imperialist power whose citizens were much worse off than their Soviet counterparts.

As noted, the exhibit was shown annually in six Soviet cities, divided into two six-month tours of duty. I served on the second "shift" of this exhibit in 1972, which was shown from July through December in the cities of Kazan, Donetsk, and Leningrad (now Saint Petersburg).

At the close of the exhibit in each city, we would pack the items into crates, and Soviet workers would load them into large containers and then onto trains for transport to the next city. During the two-week hiatus this created, we had the opportunity to travel to various parts of the USSR—with the permission, of course, of the Soviet Government. We carried "official" US government passports, meaning that we needed an exit visa to leave the Soviet Union. Only those carrying "diplomatic" passports could freely cross international boundaries without a visa.

I was able to visit a total of six additional cities while "on leave" between exhibit sites.[3] This added to the breadth and depth of my exposure to life in the Soviet Union of 1972—an experience I wouldn't care to repeat, but one that helped me in

---

2. Such products were luxury items in the old Soviet Union and were only available to members of the Communist Party and to Soviet officials.
3. These included three trips through Moscow and side trips to Riga, Tallinn, Sochi, Odessa, and Kiev.

many ways. My linguistic abilities were enhanced, as was my knowledge of the USSR and of Communism.

Included in the following chapters are some samples of the hundreds of photographs I took during my trip, accompanied with brief explanatory captions. These expand upon the information contained in the book and are included to provide visual augmentation to the narrative of the text.

Hopefully this book will give you, the reader, a glimpse of the Soviet Union of forty-five years ago, as well as a feel for life in a place where a huge all-powerful central government rules every aspect of life. Although the Soviet Union has passed into history, the world still contains places where this model of society and governance endure. A basic understanding of this system provides a backdrop for evaluating it in today's world and can help free men and women make informed choices based on historical facts and irrefutable evidence.

PREPARING FOR THE JOURNEY

If we were to promise people nothing but revolution,
they would scratch their heads and say:
"Is it not better to have good goulash?"
—Nikita Khrushchev

Before traveling to the Soviet Union, those who would man the stands of the *Research and Development in the USA* exhibit had to be properly trained, not only as to the specific items to be on display, but also as to the various realities of what would await us in the USSR. This involved two weeks of rather intense training and preparation in Washington, DC.

We were housed in the beautiful old Roger Smith Hotel, which is located at Eighteenth Street and Pennsylvania Avenue NW. This grandiose structure, built in 1911, had one of the finest dining facilities in the city. Located one block from the White House, it was the nearest hotel to the State Department building where our training was held.

The rooms in the Roger Smith were very nice. They were spacious, air-conditioned, and somewhat fancy. We even had maid service every day. Quite a difference from the modest apartment I had called home during my final two years at Kent State University. Apparently we were going to be treated in style, almost like real diplomats. Until we arrived in Moscow, that is.

During this period, we attended lectures by USIA security personnel describing what our daily lives were going to be like in the USSR. Here we learned that the Soviets basically tolerated the USIA exhibit program, but that there was no love lost on their part for us. And we were going to have to be on the lookout wherever we went. The Soviet secret police—the KGB[1]—was very powerful, and their presence was felt at all times by everyone throughout the USSR.

It was explained to us that we would carry "official" US government passports. These differed from diplomatic passports in some crucially important ways. First, our "red cover" passports (as opposed to the black covered diplomatic passports) signified only that we were American citizens employed by the US government. We held no diplomatic immunity, so any trouble we might get ourselves into in the USSR would be our own tough luck since the privileges and protections afforded to diplomats would not apply to us.

Perhaps the most significant difference between these passports was the fact that holders of the black diplomatic passports could freely travel across international borders. We red-covered-official-passport holders, however, required visas to travel. That meant we needed a Soviet entry visa to enter the USSR as well as permission to travel within the country and, ultimately, an exit visa to leave the country.

I would later come to believe we were issued only "official" passports because, in the event that some guide decided that he or she had tired of Soviet "hospitality" after, say, the first exhibit city (two months into the six-month tour of duty) and wanted to go home, this would not be possible without the permission of both the US and Soviet governments. Some of our folks would come to view these restrictions as a kind of indentured servitude, if you will.

We were briefed on the reality that the rooms we would occupy in the various hotels in the USSR would be bugged. Microphones in the walls and in the phone systems would pick up everything we said. Miniature cameras were installed in most rooms and some also had full-length mirrors near the door

---

1. The Soviet KGB (in Russian the *Komitet Gosudarstvennoi Bezopasnosti*)—the Committee for State Security—was the most powerful and feared agency of the Soviet Government. They spied on everyone in the USSR, and their tentacles reached deep into all aspects of Soviet life.

through which cameras could photograph one's every movement.

We were also told to get used to complete, round-the-clock surveillance for the entire duration of the trip upon which we were about to embark. Toward the end of our tour of duty, we developed a knack for identifying Soviet agents "shadowing" us on the street as they switched off coverage to the next agent, who would then follow us everywhere we went outside our hotels.

Sometimes this was quite easy to do as many of these folks wore the stereotypical black leather jackets commonly associated with secret policemen. At other times, we would notice a fellow behind us who would abruptly stop each time we'd pause to look through a store window or just to look around at the scenery. Over time, many of us just seemed to develop a sixth sense as to being followed.

And there would be provocations. Some would occur outside the exhibit hall. For example, the Soviets ran many scams directed at foreigners. One involved phony black market sales of "prohibited" items such as Russian Orthodox Church icons—considered to be, for these purposes, "national treasures of the state." These scams were used to fleece foreign tourists since the "prohibited" items would be confiscated by customs officials and later resold time and again to unsuspecting tourists. This type of scam could also be used to compromise officials, such as us, for the purposes of blackmail or to embarrass the American government.

We were warned that there would also be attempts at seduction by gorgeous young Russian girls—all KGB agents, of course. It seems that there existed at that time a Soviet law whereby if a foreigner were to impregnate a Soviet female, he could be held against his will in the Soviet Union until the child he had fathered turned eighteen years of age. Yikes! That was sufficient to dissuade most of the men in our group to abstain from such activities until returning home.

And there were the oceans of vodka that our people often had to consume at official gatherings such as the dinners held at the opening and closing of our exhibits in each city we visited.

We were told to be careful about alcohol consumption because it impairs judgment and can lead to embarrassing and compromising situations. In preparing to attend such events, one of our exhibit directors even went to the length of drinking a glass of olive oil, which helped the alcohol pass through his system without being fully absorbed. Or so he claimed.

There would also be provocations on the exhibit floor. Since these exhibits attracted very large crowds of Soviet visitors every day, there were all sorts of conversations that could emanate from interacting with us, since we all spoke Russian. We were told that the Soviets always salted among the visitors their agents—whom many of us called "plants"—whose job was to monitor all the conversations between us and the visitors and step in anytime things "got out of hand," meaning anytime a discussion turned to a potentially embarrassing political topic.

In this way, the Soviet Government wanted to limit the amount of genuine dialogue on topics other than those dealing directly with the items on display at the exhibit. As it turned out, these "plants" were very easy to spot, even by us, not to mention by the Soviet visitors. Whenever a conversation got interesting, the plants would shout at the guide something like "Yes, but you discriminate against black people," or "Why is your government killing babies in Vietnam?" This was a subtle signal to the Soviets at the exhibit that the conversation in which they were engaged was detrimental to the interests of the Soviet state, and that if they knew what was good for them, they would quietly walk away to another area of the exhibit.

Our Washington training also involved learning about the items we would be displaying. The array of products that comprised our exhibit ranged from small, simple gadgets such as electric mixers, knives, coffeemakers, etc. to larger items such as automobiles, a huge old Univac computer complex, and even the command module of the Apollo 10 spacecraft that stood outside the entrance to the exhibit pavilions.

In order to prepare us for the thousands of questions the visitors to the exhibit were most likely to ask, we were provided with mountains of product information. This included, among other things, the relative price of each item (along with its approximate cost in Soviet rubles) and technical details of production. For example, we would study statistical data indicating roughly how many of this or that product had been manufactured in the United States over the preceding two or three years.

The most important manufacturing and technical information concerned the three automobiles we transported to the USSR for this exhibit. To provide a representative cross section of American cars, we displayed three recently manufactured vehicles: a small Ford Pinto hatchback, an American Motors sports car (the Javelin), and a luxury Lincoln Continental.

These cars were by far the most popular of all the items and products on display, and we had to study production statistics, cost and price data, and other information about these cars in particular and the US automotive industry in general. The Soviet visitors wanted to know literally everything about these vehicles, as will be discussed in some of the following chapters.

We guides had varying degrees of proficiency in Russian. So, some of our training also included providing Russian language equivalents for things like "electric mixer" since such terms were not listed in standard Soviet dictionaries of the day. Nor were they likely to be available to the average Soviet consumer. Our training also included some visits to various facilities to witness how some of the products of American industry were manufactured. This was necessary because, as we were to find out later, the range of questions concerning the products on display was staggering.

It should be noted that learning Russian terminology for the myriad of products we were exhibiting was no small chore. This was, nevertheless, very important since the various commercial items we were displaying were available to the average American household, but not to the average Soviet citizen. And while there is precious little about which I would agree on with Frank Zappa, I am more and more convinced he was right in noting that "Communism doesn't work because people like to own stuff."

The Soviet economy was light years behind America's, at least in the consumer goods sector. The Soviet Government spent so much of its national treasure on heavy industry, the military, and maintaining its vast police state that not much was left to provide the creature comforts of everyday life for the average citizen.

In my case, I also had to study some basic computer terminology in Russian and German. I was given this assignment because I had recently graduated from college with a double major in Russian and German. I had also spent time in Germany during my military tour of duty. There was a need for someone to translate between Russian and German because Univac sent German technicians to set up and run the large computer we had. They were dispatched from Univac's subsidiaries in West Germany. As it turned out, each of the showings (in Kazan, Donetsk, and Leningrad) was staffed by a different technician because Univac apparently felt that six weeks in the Soviet Union for each of their technicians was more than enough.

Quite a number of the Soviet visitors to our exhibits in 1972 vividly remembered the German invasion of the USSR in 1941. The presence of the computer technicians from West Germany—which the Soviet Government held to be the "bad" Germany—would provide some very interesting moments, which I will describe in the following chapters. My job working that "stand" was to field questions about the computer in Russian, translate them into German, and translate the German technician's answer back into Russian for the visitors. This would prove quite challenging for me since I had virtually no computer background.

Our training also included routine matters such as being sure to take a hot plate with us to make tea for ourselves in our hotel rooms. Other subjects included things like the exchange rate between the US dollar and the Soviet ruble. This would turn out to be a very interesting matter when we actually got to our first exhibit city—Kazan. More about that later.

We also familiarized ourselves with the routine that we would follow. Toward the end of our Washington training, the *Research and Development in the USA* exhibit was about to close in the final of the three cities that had comprised its first six months (Moscow, Tbilisi, and Volgograd), and the contents were about to be transported to Kazan—the first of the three cities of the second six months of the exhibit.

Our routine was to be as follows: We would report to the first city (Kazan) roughly two weeks prior to its opening and help unpack the exhibit items from the crates used to transport them by rail. Next, we would help set up the exhibit in the pavilion. We would then display the items daily for a month, after which we would help dismantle the entire exhibit and load it back into crates for shipment to the second city. During that transportation time, we were allowed to travel to other Soviet cities according to an approved itinerary. Then we would report to the next exhibit city and the process would be repeated.

The extent and duration of our training in Washington was limited by time restrictions. But it would turn out to suffice for us to at least get started in country and get our feet wet at the first of our exhibit stops. The USIA personnel conducting the training had traveled to the Soviet Union—some many times—and eagerly shared their in-country experiences. This helped us prepare mentally and psychologically for the challenges we would face in the USSR.

We were now ready to travel to Wonderland. Well, as ready as a group of young Americans who had never been behind the Iron Curtain could be. What actually awaited us was rather shocking, even for those of us who had studied the Soviet Union in college.

It is said that the most difficult thing for college football players transitioning to the NFL is getting used to the speed of the game. One can thoroughly coach and prepare young players coming out of college for their first professional football game, but rookies really can't appreciate the difference between the speed of college games and that of NFL games until the lights go on and the whistle blows to start their first regular season game.

We were about to experience a "speed of the game" phenomenon in the Soviet Union. It was quite different from anything most of us had ever experienced. To borrow a line from the US Air Force, off we were about to go, "into the wild blue yonder."

ARRIVAL IN MOSCOW

"But I don't want to go among mad people," Alice remarked.
"Oh, you can't help that," said the Cat:
"We're all mad here.
I'm mad. You're mad."
"How do you know I'm mad?" said Alice.
"You must be," said the Cat,
"or you wouldn't have come here."
—from Lewis Carroll's *Alice in Wonderland*

Our first stop in the USSR would be Moscow. President Richard Nixon had visited Moscow in May of 1972 for a week of summit meetings with Soviet leader Leonid Brezhnev. On May 26, Nixon and Brezhnev signed the first Strategic Arms Limitation Talks Agreement (SALT I)—a treaty sources say the Soviets very much wanted, especially after Nixon's visit to China just one month before, which had resulted in the first Sino-American agreement since the 1940s.[1] There would be many interesting occurrences over the coming six months concerning China, as the average Soviet citizen was truly on edge about the China situation. I came to call it CDS—China Dread Syndrome.

We would be arriving in Moscow roughly a month after Mr. Nixon had departed. The new "détente" between the USA and the Soviet Union provided an interesting backdrop for our arrival and for the atmosphere at our exhibit during the remainder of

---

1. The Shanghai Communique of February 27, 1972, reopened direct communications between Communist China and the USA and was viewed with no small amount of trepidation by the Soviet leadership. Relations between the two Communist superpowers had been strained for quite some time and were worsening by the year.

1972. After a brief stop at Heathrow Airport in London, it was off to Moscow via the old British Overseas Airways Corporation (BOAC). As I recall, the flight lasted some four hours and landed in Moscow without incident on July 3, 1972.

We deplaned down a stairway and walked about fifty yards to the airport terminal. To be honest, I can't recall after forty-five years which of Moscow's three airports we arrived at. But I vividly remember the scene as we approached the terminal building. We had to pass through an archway, at either side of which stood grim-faced Soviet soldiers with locked and loaded AK-47 automatic rifles. By their green epaulets, I knew they were border guard troops. To be sure, these weren't like your American border-patrol folks, but stern young soldiers with a strictly business appearance. I remember looking down while approaching them, not wanting to make eye contact. One definitely doesn't want to attract undue attention from guys like this.

Clearing customs turned out to be easier than I had envisioned. Based on our training, we expected this to be a lengthy and uncomfortable process with the customs officials rummaging through every square inch of our luggage in search of whatever they might find, such as miniature spy cameras or contraband of any sort. But they had doubtless processed thousands of foreigners and knew full well that we posed no threat to Soviet national security. I breathed a sigh of relief when they quickly waved us through after a cursory inspection of our bags.

After clearing customs, we proceeded down a short corridor that led to a huge waiting room. It had to have been some fifty by seventy-five yards in size. Here I was treated to my first "eyes on" view of Soviet society. The first sensation I encountered was a tremendous amount of clamor. The entire area reminded me of a huge echo chamber, with loud shouting and an incredible sensation of semi-chaotic hustle and bustle.

The area was filled with a large number of Soviet laborers all dressed in dark blue jumpsuits. They were busily scurrying about the area looking for bags to load onto their carts, often bumping into each other, dropping items off the carts and picking them up again, and loudly shouting Russian expletives at each other. The decibel level was astounding, and this was but the first of many instances of it that I would encounter over the next six months in the Soviet Union.

I chuckled to myself, recalling times when one just couldn't find what used to be called "sky caps" to help with luggage at some of America's larger airports. What unfolded before me in Moscow was exactly the opposite. There seemed to be about fifty workers performing duties that could probably have been handled by ten or fifteen people in the West. I wondered if this was perhaps a result of the Soviet Constitution's guarantee that (among other "rights" that existed solely on paper) their citizens all had a "right to a job." At any rate, it was my first experience with a phenomenon that might be called overemployment. It would not be my last glimpse of this, either.

Our luggage was finally secured and loaded onto a large bus waiting to transport us into the city to the hotel where we would spend a couple of days in Moscow prior to heading out to our first exhibit city. It was then that we had our first encounter with representatives of Intourist.[2] They would serve as tour guides during several of our trips around the USSR.

These folks seemed somewhat surprised when we spoke Russian with them. It seemed to make them uneasy. They were clearly accustomed to explaining things to foreign tourists in the native languages of the latter. I got the feeling they would have preferred to present the Soviet version of anything seen rather than deal with foreigners who could examine things for themselves and interact directly with Soviet citizens in the Russian language.

We were taken to the Metropol Hotel in the center of the city. Built in 1905, it was a classic old structure that had been

---

2. Intourist was a Soviet contraction for *Inostrannyi Turist*, or "Foreign Tourist"—the agency that dealt with and made all arrangements in country for all foreigners and operated all Soviet hotels where foreigners were authorized to stay. They arranged for transporting us as a group to hotels and on "field trips" in the various cities we visited.

remarkably well preserved. I recall being impressed with the number of thick carpets in the hallways and the Versailles parquet design of the hardwood floors in the guest rooms. I was surprised to find that we each had a separate room here, unlike what would be the case in the cities where our exhibit was to be shown. There we would be paired off, two to a room.

The check-in process was another small eye-opener for me. Unlike the very friendly customer-service-oriented hotel personnel in the United States, the folks manning the reception desk at the Metropol were, to be kind, less than cheery. One even barked an order at a member of our group—a characteristic of Soviet hospitality employees to which we would all become quite accustomed over time.

It was here that we were also introduced to the Soviet concept of maids. Not the friendliest people I had ever encountered, these ladies had duties to perform far beyond the run-of-the-mill housekeeping. Each floor of every Intourist hotel of that era had a supervisory maid assigned to keep tabs on the guests. She ran the floor as if it were her own personal division of the Soviet Government. I recall greeting our floor's super maid in polite Russian, only to receive a scowl and a grunt in return. *Nice,* I thought.

After checking in and settling into our rooms, three of us set about exploring our new accommodations. The Metropol had a large dining facility as well as a "tea room," which was really just a smaller version of the main restaurant, with a limited menu. We decided to head down to the tea room for some libations and a bite to eat. It was here that I was introduced to the kabuki dance known as dining in Soviet restaurants.

A middle-aged stone-faced waiter whisked by our table and dropped off three menus. The choices were limited to what the Russians call *zakuski* (snacks), which are traditionally consumed while drinking vodka. After about a twenty-minute wait, the waiter finally reappeared and asked gruffly, "What do you want?"

Here I was to learn an important lesson about dining in the USSR. Quite often the menu contained items that were sold out. As we ordered each such item, the waiter would interrupt with

"*Nyetu* [Don't have any]," and we would select another item. After we had played this game for about five minutes and finally found something that was available, the waiter then snapped up the menus and said, "Anything to drink?"

I answered, "Vodka."

He replied, "How much?" I said something like "a glass for each of us," prompting him to snort and yell, "How many grams?"

Now I was in deep waters. During my two years of military service in Germany, we ordered beer in liters or fractions thereof. But grams? I had no clue as to how many grams were in an ounce or vice versa. So, I blurted out in Russian, "Fifty grams," which would be the equivalent of about two ounces of vodka.

The waiter laughed loudly and snarled, "For three people? What, are you going to drink out of thimbles?" So, I asked his advice as to how much we should order. He grunted and said, "Minimum two hundred fifty." I said that would be fine and he dashed off.

This wasn't going to be so easy after all. The "speed of the game" had just ramped up.

The next day was the Fourth of July. We had been informed by our staff of a longstanding tradition in Moscow whereby the American ambassador would host a party in honor of America's birthday. So, off we went to the reception at Spaso House—the ambassador's residence in the Soviet Union.

Judging by the portion of this facility that we viewed while passing through toward the reception area, it had the air of another old, very classy domicile. The rear door opened into a quiet, walled-off courtyard where tables and a bar had been set up. The ambassador traditionally invited all American officials in Moscow to this reception, as well as high-ranking members of the Soviet Foreign Service—people whom George Orwell perhaps had in mind as being "more equal than others" in a land of supposed equality.

The most interesting Soviet guest at the reception that day was Viktor Sukhodrev, the personal interpreter for the Soviet leadership. I noticed that he was dressed in an expensive-looking suit with a flashy tie and looked the part of a member of the

Soviet hierarchy. He was quite glib and very interesting to talk to. As he interacted with members of our group, I thought to myself that here was a man who frequently walked the halls of the Kremlin alongside the most powerful leaders of the USSR. He exuded an aura of poise and confidence and was very well spoken in English.

I had seen Sukhodrev before. He had almost perfect control of English, and his pronunciation was excellent. At a 1967 summit with President Lyndon Johnson in Glassboro, New Jersey, he translated Alexei Kosygin's remarks into virtually flawless Standard American English. Kosygin also stopped in London on his way home, and his visit there was also televised. My jaw dropped when I watched this same Sukhodrev translate Kosygin's remarks into impeccable British English.[3]

The chance to dialogue with such a superb linguist and one with such an interesting background was quite an opportunity for us since we all had college degrees in Russian. Our small group gathered around Sukhodrev and asked him several questions, many of which dealt with foreign-language learning in the USSR.

At one point, I asked him, "Mr. Sukhodrev, I notice you did not mention Chinese as one of the primary foreign languages taught in the Soviet Union and was wondering why not."

Sukhodrev smiled wryly and, with a bit of humor in his voice, said, "Well, we're still quite optimistic."

There it was: another example of the effects of China Dread Syndrome—this time coming from a person with connections to the highest leaders of the Soviet Union.

During our brief stay in Moscow, we made several trips to the American embassy, which, in those years, was located on Tchaikovsky Street near the city center. It was a very old, almost

---

3. Only later did I learn that Sukhodrev's father had served in Soviet Intelligence in the United States. Also, young Viktor had spent six years in London, where his mother worked at the Soviet trade mission. Sukhodrev had attended a school for children of Soviet diplomats in London. He was the personal translator and interpreter for a number of Soviet leaders, including Nikita Khrushchev, Alexei Kosygin, Leonid Brezhnev, and, briefly, Mikhail Gorbachev.

foreboding facility. There was very little traffic on the street, and the entrance to the embassy was through an archway, at either side of which stood grim-faced uniformed Soviet policemen. Their function was apparently to ensure that no Soviet citizens gained access to the embassy. Soviet officials took a dim view of defections and other anti-Soviet behavior. In addition to the uniformed police, there were always several plainclothes officers and KGB types mulling about, smoking and watching. They were easily identifiable to Soviet citizens, and the message was clear: Don't come near this facility. We had to show our American passports to enter.

The embassy housed a commissary facility where American food was available. The food was nothing special, but I recall the bacon-and-egg breakfasts and the hamburgers on the lunch menu. This might appear somewhat mundane and of little interest except for the fact that this was the only place in the USSR where good old-fashioned American chow was available. The embassy was also the facility through which we would send and receive personal letters delivered by courier to and from our remote cities. It was, in short, our link to the outside world, and I frequented it every time I was in Moscow.

On the morning of July 5, while walking to the US embassy to have breakfast, we passed by the large Soviet bookstore *Dom Knigi* and witnessed a sight that gave me another interesting glimpse of daily life in the USSR. A line had formed, probably hours before, and we learned from one man standing in the long line that some new book had come out and people wanted to get a copy before it sold out. Russians are voracious readers, and word of the publication of new books always spread rapidly through the capital.

After a scrumptious breakfast, a couple of us attended to some personal business at the embassy and then set off on foot back to the Metropol. Approaching *Dom Knigi*, we noticed the line was still quite long. As we walked by, the service window through which the new book was being distributed suddenly slammed shut. A sign was hung out that read Sold Out. I would wager that some folks had been standing in that line for three hours, if not longer.

Had this happened at an American store, there would likely have been a loud commotion and quite a bit of grousing. Astonishingly, the Soviets who had been standing in line all this time simply shrugged it off and silently went on their way. This was one of my first clues as to what the Soviet people had to endure due to shortages of a variety of consumer products. But books, too? My friend and I just looked at each other and shrugged our shoulders. This would not be the last time we would see similar reactions in situations such as this in Soviet Wonderland.

The short time we were in Moscow as a brief stopover on our way to Kazan did not allow for much sightseeing. A few of us did go over to the famous Red Square, but I decided not to spend the time it would take to go to Lenin's Mausoleum. That could be done on another trip through Moscow.

On July 6, our group was bused to the airport for our flight to Kazan, where we would begin our duties as guides on the American cultural exchange exhibit, *Research and Development in the USA*. This time we were accompanied by a young woman who worked for the *Torgovaya Palata*—the Soviet Chamber of Commerce.[4] We'll call her *Masha*. Over the coming months we would come to get to know her rather well.

Masha was a typical Soviet official and a classic example of what the Soviet system had produced. She was all business with no sense of humor, a rigid Communist ideologue, and routinely took offense at any suggestion that life in the USSR was anything short of idyllic. No one dared tell a joke around her, and we were very careful as to what we said in her presence. Another representative of the *Torgovaya Palata* once told me that he, too,

---

4. Actually, this was the official term used by the Soviets. This organization was radically different from an American chamber of commerce. They were actually working for the Soviet secret police—the KGB—and their job was to ensure that we didn't stray into prohibited areas and to keep tabs on us throughout our stay in the USSR, both in the cities where the exhibit was shown and during our vacation trips inside the country.

was very circumspect in his interactions with her and avoided her whenever possible. Masha involuntarily helped me to experience what it felt like to be a Soviet citizen since she seemed to be continuously watching us and no doubt reported our every action to her superiors.

The flight to Kazan was my first experience with the Soviet national airline Aeroflot. It is difficult to put into words the difference between Aeroflot and any American airline. Back in the day, the latter treated passengers as valued customers, whereas the former more closely resembled an operation roughly approximating the herding of livestock.

In the 1970s, the Aeroflot fleet consisted mainly of rather old aircraft—mostly various models of the Ilyushin design. The seats were metal and there were few, if any, creature comforts on board. Although Masha insisted that Comrade Leonid Brezhnev himself flew on the same model of the Ilyushin fleet as our plane from Moscow to Kazan, I silently thought that if this were true, the leader of the Communist Party of the Soviet Union must be a masochist.

We boarded the plane and took our seats. And then we waited. And waited. And waited. It was very hot in the aircraft's cabin. It was, after all, July. In those days, the cabin was not pressurized until just before takeoff, so we sat sweltering for about twenty minutes until the engines were fired up and the air vents above us began blowing cool air.

As we began taxiing out to the runway, I noticed that one of the turboprop engines on my side of the plane seemed to be leaking a black liquid ominously resembling oil. No use fretting about it. The only option was to buckle up, sit back, and hope. The ride was pretty bumpy, and we later learned that many Soviet commercial pilots of that era had earned their wings in the Soviet Air Force—many during World War II. That explained the rather sudden turns and other airborne maneuvers that one doesn't experience when flying United or American Airlines back home. There would come a time later in our stay when several of us decided that it would be more prudent to travel by train.

But, as this was our first trip inside the Soviet Union, we just sat back and settled in for the ninety-minute, 450-mile flight to Kazan. No one talked much during the flight. Conversation would have been virtually impossible anyway since the din inside the plane was deafening and one couldn't hear what the person next to him was saying.

As we approached the Kazan airport, I thought, *Well, pretty soon it'll be "show time."*

A view of the Kremlin in Moscow—the seat of Soviet power in the 1970s. It still houses the offices of the highest levels of today's government of the Russian Federation.

The Moscow Kremlin houses beautiful churches—reminders of the power and authority of the Russian Orthodox Church prior to the 1917 Russian Revolution.

Moscow's famous Red Square. This photo shows Saint Basil's Cathedral on the left, the famous Spasskaya Tower to its right, Lenin's Mausoleum on the right, and the Kremlin Wall behind it.

The great Kremlin Wall with governmental offices and three famous Russian Orthodox churches on the grounds of the Kremlin.

The Cathedral of Vasily the Blessed, commonly known as Saint Basil's Cathedral, on Red Square. This magnificent edifice, completed in 1561, was built over a six-year period on orders from Tsar Ivan IV (Ivan the Terrible) to commemorate the Russian capture of Kazan and Astrakhan. According to an ancient legend, Tsar Ivan ordered the eyes of the architect to be poked out so that he could never replicate the grandeur of this gorgeous structure.

A closer view of Saint Basil's, showing the monument dedicated to Prince Dmitri Pozharsky and a commoner, Kuzma Minin. It celebrated the seventeenth-century liberation of Moscow from Poland by armies under the command of these two historic figures of Russian history. This is the monument referred to in a subsequent chapter entitled "On the Lighter Side."

KAZAN

This city is undoubtedly the first in Russia after Moscow;
every little thing shows that Kazan
is the capital of a large kingdom.
— eighteenth-century Russian Empress Catherine II
(1762–96)

ARRIVAL IN KAZAN

Our flight to Kazan, bumpy and noisy as it was, came to an uneventful end with a fairly smooth landing at the relatively small Kazan airport on July 6. It turned out that the oil or whatever was leaking from the plane did not amount to anything significant after all. My ears were still ringing from the ninety-minute flight as we descended from the Ilyushin aircraft and proceeded to the terminal. On our way to retrieve our luggage, my thoughts again turned to the approach of "show time," which would ensue in just a few days.

It is rumored that the name *Kazan* is an ancient Tatar word meaning "cauldron." Judging by the temperature in July and August, we certainly felt like we were in a very hot cauldron. This city, located on the Volga River, was founded some 950 years before our arrival. As with several old cities in the domain of the Russian Empire, Kazan had its own "kremlin."[1] In 1972, the city retained much of its antiquity, and little of today's modernity was in evidence.

We made the short trip by bus from the Kazan airport to our hotel, the Hotel Volga.[2] Located about a hundred yards from the

---

1. The Russian word *kreml'* means "a fortified citadel." When capitalized (*Kreml'*), it refers to the Moscow Kremlin.

Volga River, it had seen its better days. This was definitely not the Metropol. The carpets were rather frayed and the furniture in the small lobby appeared to have been stitched up more than a few times. The only feature even remotely similar to the classy Moscow hotel was the crisscross design in the wooden floors of the guest rooms.

Needless to say, there was nothing resembling air-conditioning in the rooms. Thanks to the July heat, one of the first things I did after settling into my room was open the faucet in the tiny "bathroom" (quotation marks intentional) to wash my sweaty face. To my astonishment, the tap water came out a light green color. God only knows how old the plumbing in the hotel was. I would boil all water for drinking and even for brushing my teeth for the next six months.

Our hotel was just across the street from one of the main rail lines going through Kazan. We would find this a source of irritation since quite a few trains passed through the city—many of them in the dead of night. Some "local" trains were still pulled by steam engines in 1972, and they made quite a racket. Due to the heat (around one hundred degrees in July) and the lack of air-conditioning in the rooms, we tried to keep the windows open, at least at night, despite the noise of the trains. But open windows created yet another problem. The windows had no screens. During our first evening in Kazan, my roommate and I headed down to eat at the hotel restaurant, leaving the windows in our room open and the lights on. With the river so close and the heat so high, we returned an hour later to find bugs all over our room. Some were so large I think we could have put saddles on them and ridden them around.

We were paired off, two to a room. According to my notes from the period, each of us paid nine rubles per day for these accommodations. Noticing that the price was listed in the lobby as three rubles per day, I quickly understood that the price we were paying was the "foreigner rate." Any Soviet guest could

2. The description of the Hotel Volga in this book deals with the old Soviet version of the facility. Since that time, it has undergone a major renovation and is now a much different and better entity than we knew in 1972.

rent the same room for one third of what *each* of us was being charged. This amounted to eighteen rubles per day for the double room. I thought, *Nice job of negotiating our room rates, State Department.*

What made things worse was that we were required to pay the hotel bill by check in US dollars. On the open market at that time, a dollar was worth about four Soviet rubles. But when it came time to write the check, it had to be written according to the "official" rate of exchange agreed upon by our State Department "experts"—$1.25 for each ruble. So, had we been allowed to pay the regular Soviet room rate using anything resembling a fair ruble-to-dollar exchange rate, each of us would have paid around $5 weekly, rather than the $78 amount extracted from us each week. Bad enough for each of us, but even worse for the American taxpayer since the government was paying us a per diem allowance to cover this expense.

Another feature of our hotel room presented an "aha" moment for me. In one corner of the room was a shelf upon which stood a small radio. I decided to see what stations I could tune in to, but when I turned it on, there were only two options: "on" and "off." The only program one could listen to on this radio (and on most others in the USSR at that time) was Radio Moscow in Russian. But, then again, why would anyone need any other source for news?

WALKING AROUND THE CITY

During the few days before setting up our equipment at the exhibit pavilion, we had the chance to do some sightseeing, including of the old citadel, the Kazan Kremlin. As I walked around the city, I took several photographs—something that would become a routine for me at each stop we made during my six-month journey in the USSR. Some of these appear at the end of the various chapters of this book.

One day a friend and I happened to come across an old church named in honor of a Russian saint, *Nikolai Chudotvorets*—Saint Nicholas the Miracle Worker. As we would learn, this was one of very few "working" churches in Kazan in 1972. Unfortunately, we could not enter the building because there were no services in progress at the time of our visit.

There were, however, a few elderly Russians sitting on benches and on the steps at the entrance to the church, and we were able to strike up a conversation with some of them. The men sported long beards, and the women were clad in the traditional Russian head scarves. When we told them that we were from America, their ears perked up right away. Not surprisingly, they began peppering us with questions. These folks were genuinely astounded that two young Americans had mysteriously appeared out of nowhere and were speaking Russian with them, not to mention their amazement to learn that we, like they, believed in God. I wondered if this intense questioning was a preview of what our work at the exhibit was going to be like.

Back in the 1950s, Nikita Khrushchev had famously said that religion was fading away in the USSR, as evidenced (he claimed) by the fact that only old women attended church services. Of course, he failed to note that each successive generation of elderly Russian churchgoers was followed by another, and another, and another. The ladies we spoke with at the church in Kazan had been taught religion at home by their mothers and grandmothers, and I thought while talking to them that they had probably been doing likewise with their daughters and granddaughters.

During another excursion around Kazan, I came across an older gentleman sitting on a park bench. I sat down next to him, introduced myself as an American who would be working at the exhibit in Kazan, and struck up a conversation with him. Without intending any disrespect, I casually remarked that the city had the appearance of being rather old, at which time the aged gentleman looked down at a badly buckled sidewalk, peered out into the street, which was in some disrepair, and said in a wry voice, "Well, you must remember that the Germans didn't get this far."

This was the fellow's sarcastic way of complaining about the lack of Soviet effort at that time to modernize the city. He was referring to the fact that the areas of the Soviet Union invaded and occupied by the German Army in World War II had suffered such incredible damage that many of them had to be almost completely rebuilt. Kazan was thus not a rebuilding priority.

Within a couple of days of our arrival in Kazan, the local authorities issued and distributed to our group a list of the bus and trolley lines in the city showing stops beyond which we would not be permitted to travel. I wondered at the time what it was they might be hiding, but then remembered my conversation with the old fellow about Kazan's age. Perhaps there were worse signs of age and neglect than potholes and buckled sidewalks—things the Soviets didn't want us to see, let alone photograph.

All in all, our "down time" prior to our exhibit getting set up was interesting and informative, but not nearly as intriguing as things we would discover when we actually began coming into contact with Soviet citizens visiting our exhibit.

SETTING UP AND PREPARING FOR THE EXHIBIT

Several days prior to the opening of the exhibit in Kazan on July 17 were spent on "setup." As previously described, the Soviets transported the exhibit by rail to each city where it was to be shown. The display items were waiting for us when we arrived, and our first real chore was to help get them unpacked and into the exhibit facility.

This would become an interesting part of our assignment in each city because it gave us the opportunity to converse with the Soviet workers assigned to do the manual labor involved in unpacking the items and helping us set them up in the exhibit hall. A pattern soon developed that greatly enhanced my experience. As it turned out, the Soviets assigned quite a few older fellows to these work details. They often sat around and told the younger laborers what to do.

This situation gave us a chance to meet and dialogue with older people who seemed to fear the regime less than the younger people did. They were often quite willing to open up and talk to us about things that the average Soviet citizen would never discuss with foreigners, especially with us—we were, after all, employees of the American government. And in 1972 the multi-decade Cold War was still quite real. As American television commentator Andy Rooney used to say, "I've learned that the best classroom in the world is at the feet of an elderly person." I came to understand the wisdom of this expression during my six-month stay in the Soviet Union.

One old gentleman told me very frankly that he wasn't afraid of the Soviet authorities in the least. He said something like "What are they going to do, send me to prison? At my age, I don't care, because I'm never going to get out of this place, anyway."

Their candor made these older folks a fountain of interesting and revealing information, and I always actively sought them out wherever we traveled throughout the Soviet Union. In Kazan, this turned out to be especially true since, prior to our arrival, the city had been a "restricted area" and thus off-limits to foreigners. This made us, as Russian-speaking Americans, a genuine rarity. I had always thought that all Soviets—regardless of age—would be afraid to speak openly with Americans. But these elderly folks tended to speak surprisingly frankly and openly with me—more so than would be the case at the exhibit itself.

One thing I learned very early on from these senior citizens was the scope of one of the USSR's most serious problems: alcoholism. This often revealed itself in the form of jokes. As I would come to understand during my time in the Soviet Union, a large number of people apparently lived on two things: vodka and jokes. I only wish I had had a portable tape recorder with me to capture the hundreds of jokes to which I was exposed as I traveled about the country.

Here's a quick example. Marxist theory held that a proletarian revolution overthrows a bourgeois capitalist regime, leading to the creation of a Socialist state that would, over time, develop into Communism. One old fellow told me the following joke concerning this theory: "Soviet social scientists recently discovered an intermediary step between Socialism and Communism—alcoholism."

I was truly astonished at the amount of alcohol consumption I witnessed in the USSR. I had seen quite a bit of drinking while in the military, especially in Germany, where beer was consumed at a much greater rate than water. But Soviet Russians—trapped inside a hermetically sealed society—had taken alcohol use to an entirely different level.

The day before "opening day" of the exhibit was a day off, which we used to again venture out into the city and explore. Around noon we came across a small outdoor kiosk where beer was sold.[3] There were three of us, and we each ordered a mug of beer. We had just sat down on a bench when I noticed a strange phenomenon. Three men approached the kiosk and ordered beer. They then proceeded to drink some of the beer from each mug, then brandished a bottle of very cheap Soviet vodka and poured some of it into each glass. This was followed by the very rapid consumption of the contents of the mug. Others near the kiosk had apparently been doing the same, and within a short time there were several very intoxicated fellows lying prostrate on the ground nearby.

Soon a police van drove up. Three officers got out, opened the rear doors of the van, and began hurling the inebriated guys into the back. The police vehicle then sped away. A few months later I learned that the publicly intoxicated were often transported to what was euphemistically called a "sobering up" place—what we would call a detox center. This was usually in the basement of a local police station, where the drunks were allowed to sleep off their stupor and were awakened by water being sprayed on them full force from a fire hose. Not exactly a genteel manner of sobering folks up, but I suppose it was effective.

Soon our rather limited "free time" ended. It was now time to get to work and earn our pay.

---

3. The Russian term for this kiosk was *pivnushka,* derived from the word *pivo,* meaning "beer" in Russian.

WORKING THE EXHIBIT

Our exhibit opened on July 17, 1972, in a geodesic dome, which I later learned had been stored somewhere in Europe for repeated usage in USIA exhibits to various countries behind the Iron Curtain. Near the entrance to the facility stood the actual command module used in the Apollo 10 mission, which had orbited the moon in 1969 with astronauts Thomas Stafford, John Young, and Eugene Cernan. Quite an impressive first item for visitors to see on their way into the dome.

Unfortunately, this dome, as with our hotel rooms, had no air-conditioning. It should be noted that during our working hours at the exhibit, we were required by the USIA to wear coats and ties, unlike the casual attire of the Soviet visitors. Throw in temperatures of up to one hundred degrees and thousands of Soviet visitors walking around the inside of the facility every hour, and you have less than ideal working conditions.

After entering the exhibit hall, the visitors were free to roam around and check out the numerous items on display. Most importantly, they had the chance to speak with us—the first foreigners the vast majority of people in Kazan had ever seen and certainly the first Americans who spoke their language. And for us—the guides—it was our first chance to interact with large numbers of Soviet citizens in their country and in their language.

Our work routine would turn out to be virtually the same in all three cities where the exhibit was to be shown. Generally speaking, we would work two hours at one of the stands—elevated platforms where the items were on display—and then get one hour off. This cycle would repeat itself throughout the work day until the exhibit closed in the late afternoon. As I recall, we worked six days on and got one day off during each of the four weeks the exhibit was open in each city. It was a fairly grueling schedule, but we were all young and in good health, and, after all, this was a dream come true for many of us since it was the culmination of many years of studying Russian.

As a rule, the guides would rotate among the stands displaying the wide array of products we had brought from America to show our Soviet visitors. This meant that during one hour one might be explaining the various features of some small kitchen appliances, and the next hour the same guide could be talking about one of the three cars on display. This provided a variety of scenarios for the guides and reduced the boredom one felt when working only one stand.

As previously described, most of my time was spent translating questions about our computer from Russian to German and the answers from our German technicians into Russian. It was quite a learning experience for me since computer technology had not been my forte either in college or in the military. Often, if the subject became too technical, the Soviets and our German tech would use pencil and paper to draw circuit boards and other diagrams, which served to bridge my insufficient understanding of the concepts they were discussing.

Far more interesting and productive than the descriptions of the items being displayed were the conversations that inevitably arose concerning social and political matters, and here the discussions often became quite lively. As we had been trained to expect, among the hundreds of visitors to the exhibit each hour, the Soviets had interspersed what some of us came to call "plants." These were people who could be described as professional agitators mixed in with the average citizens to make sure the dialogue didn't become too negative or even "dangerous" from the point of view of the Soviet Government.

Most of these young men were usually unrecognizable as secret police plants as far as their clothing or general mannerisms were concerned. But we were quickly able to identify them as soon as they began interrupting us in loud and authoritative voices. The Soviet visitors immediately knew who they were and why they were there. Again, no potentially anti-Soviet thoughts or ideas were to be tolerated, especially in the presence of foreigners. The monolithic control over Soviet society enforced by the Communist Party and the regime had to be maintained at all costs. The very idea that positions dealing with political or ideological matters that failed to completely conform to—much less directly confront—official Soviet propaganda were viewed

by the Soviet authorities as taboo. It was what they feared most
about direct interaction between us and their citizens.

It was noteworthy that when discussions turned in this
direction, large crowds would gather in front of the stand where
such matters were being raised and "debated," as it were. This
was a signal to the plants to get over to that area of the exhibit
floor and, where necessary, get directly involved in squelching
any potentially controversial discussions.

They employed various methods to achieve this. Sometimes
the plant would interject Soviet propaganda directly into the
conversation. Another ploy they used was to loudly say
something like "Enough about politics. Tell me how this gadget
works," pointing to an item on display. Both tactics often had the
effect of stifling debate and dispersing the crowd. The visitors
clearly understood that one or more of them had entered a
"forbidden area" of discourse and that they'd better move along
and stop talking about things the government didn't want
discussed openly with Americans.

As Kazan was the first of our exhibit cities, we experienced, at
least initially, some difficulty in dealing with such Soviet tactics.
But, as they say, practice makes perfect. As the days and weeks
wore on, most of us developed creative ways of fending off the
Soviet propaganda and getting our points across to the visitors.

It was apparent from the earliest days of our work at the
exhibit that the plants were quite well briefed on every social
problem in America, from unemployment to racial strife, to the
Vietnam War and the so-called peace movement, to crime, to
student demonstrations, to name but a few. Many would treat
these issues as a battering ram to illustrate for the Soviet public
how evil America was as compared to the "Socialist paradise" in
which they lived in the USSR.

Several amusing instances come to mind as illustrative of
how some guides dealt with this phenomenon. Here are some
examples.

Toward the middle of our time in Kazan, one plant had been
working one of our guides over about several of the
aforementioned issues. When he got to the matter of

unemployment, the Soviet fellow said something like "So, tell me. What is this thing called 'unemployment' which you have in America? We have no such thing in the Soviet Union."

The American guide—one of the more vocal in our group—immediately piped up and said, "I'm glad you brought that up. Actually, I'm not surprised that you have full employment in the USSR, since half your people seem to be busy watching and reporting on the other half."

This exchange was met with some snickering from the audience before they began walking away. I believe they likely felt that the young American fellow had deftly put the Soviet plant in his place, and many were probably glad he did so.

Another interesting occurrence involved our German tech working the Univac stand. After a session focusing on mostly technical questions and answers with the visitors, he and I were leaning against one of the disk drives of the large computer complex, conversing in German. A Soviet fellow who appeared somewhat inebriated walked up and abruptly said to the guy in a loud voice, "Heil Hitler," and then walked away. As he did so, the tech whispered to me in German: "My uncle used to work with quite a few Russians, and he told me that most of them were complete jerks. Looks like he may have been right."

Although I spent most of my time working the Univac stand, from time to time I managed to steal away for an hour here and there to work on what was clearly the most interesting and fun area of the exhibit—the three cars we had brought from America. At the end of each day, when closing down the exhibit hall, we could look down the row where the cars were on display and see what looked like a million fingerprints down the sides and across the hoods of these vehicles. The Soviet visitors simply couldn't get enough of them.

One day when I was working the area where the cars were on display, a young fellow asked me how many cars there were in America. I thought he was referring to annual automobile production figures, so I referred to our notebook on that subject and began reeling off the numbers. He interrupted me and said,

"No, no. I want to know how many *total* cars there are in the United States."

My reply was simply a reaction to the magnitude of the question. I blurted out, "Oh, I have no idea. I mean, how many Chinese are there in China?"

The young man turned quite pale and stammered, "Why did you mention China? I didn't say anything about China."

It immediately became clear to me that this was another instance of CDS—China Dread Syndrome. The fellow quickly vanished into the crowd and probably headed to the nearest beer kiosk for some liquid solace and to regain his composure. From this incident I also understood that I needed to refrain not only from any jokes about China, but also from even mentioning it in a hyperbolic reply to a question such as the one the young guy had asked me. It was another lesson to file in my memory bank for future use.

Around the third of our four weeks working the exhibit, we learned through our courier returning from Moscow of a serious train accident that had occurred on the Moscow-Kazan railroad line.[4] The day after learning of this event, I mentioned it to a group of Soviet visitors at the exhibit. They assured me that since neither *Pravda* nor *Izvestiya* had reported on such an incident, it clearly hadn't happened and was probably fabricated by Western intelligence sources to "slander the Soviet Union." The Soviet press simply spiked stories they deemed "not newsworthy."

And so it continued throughout our time working the exhibit in Kazan. We were settling into a routine, and by the time we reached our last week of the event, we had become fairly skillful in discussing a wide range of issues with our Soviet visitors. We had learned how to differentiate between serious questions posed by curious visitors versus the overt—and sometimes subtly hidden—barbs and provocations of those who had been "salted"

---

4. We sent our mail out by embassy courier about every two weeks. This avoided having to write letters and leave them in our rooms for the Soviets to tamper with. Upon his return, the courier would bring return mail through the US embassy in Moscow, along with news from Embassy Row—often concerning matters the Soviet press failed to report on.

among the visitors to guide otherwise open discussions away from "prohibited" topics that might prove embarrassing to the Soviet hierarchy.

The most interesting event during the Kazan exhibit took place two or three days before it was to close. A quite elderly gentleman walked up to me carrying a small mesh shopping bag that contained about eight or ten freshly picked apples. He handed it to me and told me to please accept it as a gift from an old Russian who admired the United States. Before walking away, he gave me a wink and said, "The sweetest of these apples are toward the bottom of the bag."

I thanked him and took the small bag backstage at the stand where I had been working for two hours. As I began taking out the apples, I noticed a piece of paper that had been folded up into a very small cube. I retrieved it and began unfolding the paper. To my amazement, it was a handwritten note that the old fellow had smuggled into the apple bag.[5] Here is what it read:

We have a totalitarian regime. If we had a democratic republic, we would have progressed further and achieved more. Nowadays the psychiatric hospitals are filled with dissidents. All the positive comments in your comments book are immediately torn out by the KGB. You should take pride in having such a democratic country and not be overly tolerant in the face of those who have been blinded and deceived by propaganda.

He signed it only as "a member of the Russian Social Democratic Labour Party,"—the forerunner of the Communist Party, which had split into the Bolsheviks and the Mensheviks.

By way of explanation, our staff had placed a "comments book" near the exit from the pavilion. Unfortunately, none of our staff seemed to pay much attention to this book, and the old fellow's note indicated that the remarks written in it were carefully monitored by Soviet officials, who were frequently seen walking around near the exit area. I have no doubt whatsoever that they indeed tore out any pages containing even moderately

---

5. A picture of the original note in Russian appears in the photo section at the end of this chapter.

positive remarks about our exhibit, leaving only those comments that echoed the Soviet line and would be approved by the Party.

Even at his quite advanced age, this little fellow had taken a substantial risk by sneaking his note to me. Any such action criticizing the Soviet Government and/or praising the USA in comparison to the USSR could easily have led to a charge of treason and resulted in severe punishment, even for a senior citizen. There were, after all, some things that simply were not tolerated, regardless of one's age. This explains why the man had taken great pains to fold up his note into a very small cube and insert it toward the bottom of the bag (probably after the Soviets had inspected the sack at the entrance to the hall) to avoid detection. It was yet another clear piece of evidence indicating the degree to which the Soviet people lived in constant fear of their own government, despite what their official propaganda organs in the press claimed.

A week or so before the exhibit closed, the Soviets arranged a sightseeing trip for us to travel to a youth recreational camp on the banks of the Volga River on the outskirts of Kazan. This was intended to show us how wonderful life in the USSR was for young people—swimming, hiking, and other forms of youth activities were all on display there. Of course, what we were not shown were the endless hours of political indoctrination that also took place at such youth facilities.

They bused us out of the city into the surrounding countryside along a well-paved road. In the 1970s such paved roads outside of large cities were deemed "strategic thoroughfares," meaning they had been paved for use by military transport vehicles. After reaching the surrounding areas, the presence of several unpaved (dirt) roads signified that we were "out in the sticks." The pictures in the photo section at the end of this chapter highlight the difference in the overall appearance of such areas from that of city life.

During our bus trip, we passed several old houses that looked like they could have been *dachi*.[6] Some were nice—in good repair,

6. *Dacha*, in Russian, is the word for a "country house." These were mostly for mid- to high-level Soviet officials.

freshly painted, with a nice picket fence in the front—such as one where the bus stopped and we were permitted to interact with the residents. Others appeared to be dilapidated huts, in serious disrepair and having the appearance of something out of the nineteenth century.

During this planned stop, a friend and I quietly left our group to explore the area on our own. We walked over to a nearby place, where we came across a small house surrounded by a rickety fence. An old man walked up to us and, after discovering that we were Americans, quickly rushed us through the gate and into his tiny dwelling.[7] He disappeared for a moment, then reappeared carrying a jug that had accumulated quite a bit of dust. Offering us a seat at his small table, he removed a cork from the bottle and poured each of us about two ounces of a liquid that had apparently been "aging" in the bottle for quite some time. He made a toast to his American guests, and we joined him in gulping down the contents of our glasses.

By this time in my life, I had learned how to drink straight shots of vodka. But after the liquid from this old jug cleared my oral cavity, I experienced a distinct shortness of breath. Whatever the old man had brewed up was one very strong concoction. He looked out the window, pointed to three apple trees in his yard, and said, "Apples make very good cider, don't they?"

Catching my breath, I agreed and told him that our group was probably looking for us by now and that we had to go. We thanked him for his generous hospitality and quickly rejoined our group. Our Intourist "hosts" were clearly not pleased that my friend and I had stolen off by ourselves. Our group was loaded onto the bus, and away we went back to the city. The thirty-minute return trip to Kazan was quiet and somewhat uncomfortable due to the angry looks directed at those of us who had ventured off the beaten path. The Soviets tried to keep close tabs on us during these excursions, lest we discover things we were not "authorized" to see.

---

7. I have no idea whether this man actually owned this little house, since ownership of private property was very restricted in the USSR. He simply described it as "my humble abode."

PACKING UP AND HEADING OUT

Our exhibit closed on August 17, and we set about helping the Soviet laborers place the items into crates, which were then loaded into "containers" for their rail journey to the exhibit's next stop. We basically helped with the lighter items and helped supervise the loading of the heavier ones into crates to be hoisted onto railroad flatcars for their ride south to Donetsk.

All this, of course, gave me another chance to interact with the older laborers helping get the items packed away for their journey. As always, they recounted numerous jokes about life and times in the Soviet Union.[8] They also related real-life stories about some of their experiences from growing up in the USSR in Stalin's time and, of course, during the Second World War, the official Soviet title of which was the Great Patriotic War. Several of these stories were indeed heart-wrenching, and I thought at the time how fortunate we were as Americans to live in a place that had not known hardship and deprivations of the magnitude described by these folks.

As was the custom in each of the cities where our exhibit was shown, one of the final events was a farewell dinner hosted for us by the Soviets. This dinner in Kazan was held at the hotel where we had stayed for the past several weeks and featured the traditional toasts of friendship and good wishes from the American and Soviet sides of the tables.

This event provided a final bit of ironic humor as we were preparing to leave Kazan. One of the waiters who had served us our daily meals in the hotel dining room, after consuming a bit more than his fair share of vodka, came over to me and whispered, "You know that 'beef' you guys have been ordering off the menu here during your stay? Well, actually . . ."—at which point he began to laugh and slap his hands against his thighs to the beat of galloping horse hooves. This really didn't surprise me that much since I had always found the "beef" to be a tad stringy.

---

8. To preserve space in the various chapters of this book, I decided to publish some of the more interesting and revealing Russian jokes in a later chapter entitled "On the Lighter Side." Many of these anecdotes, while being quite inventive and humorous, express how frustrating daily life was for the average Soviet citizen of the day.

This was perhaps this fellow's way of saying that in the USSR things aren't always as they seem.

I was only able to write two letters home during my stay in Kazan since the courier service was intermittent at best. Reviewing these letters some forty-five years later, I was reminded that we had to wash our own clothes, except for our shirts, which the hotel had laundered for us. Our suits would have to wait until we exited the USSR to be dry-cleaned since we had heard horror stories from embassy employees in Moscow about having suits come back missing buttons and otherwise damaged. One told of finding a tiny microphone sewn inside the lining of his suit coat.

After six long weeks in old Kazan, it was back to the airport to catch a flight to Moscow and begin our first "vacation" before reporting to our next official stop in the Ukraine. I was glad to be leaving Kazan and felt that we had been fairly successful in describing for our Soviet visitors a wide array of what life in America at that time was like. I recall hoping that at least the weather for the balance of our time would be more hospitable than the intolerable heat of Kazan.

Another quote from *Alice in Wonderland* author, Lewis Carroll, expresses what I was feeling as I departed Kazan on August 24, 1972: "I have seen so many extraordinary things, nothing seems extraordinary anymore."

These welcome signs seemed a bit odd since Kazan had long been a city where foreigners were not permitted to travel. It is possible that this sign was erected just before our arrival.

This shot from my hotel window shows another example of Soviet "overemployment." This job, involving about fifteen people, could likely have been done by seven or eight. This picture also features the Soviet version of "women's equality," whereby elderly females worked alongside men in heavy physical work.

Street scene in Kazan. Notice the scarcity of cars and the age of those on the street. As in many Soviet cities of that era, the primary means of getting around was by public conveyance. Note the trolley tracks.

An ancient citadel—the Kazan Kremlin

View of the proximity of railroad tracks to our hotel. Just beyond the row of trees is the Volga River. Local trains were still powered by steam engines in 1972. The racket they made at night was deafening.

One of our American guides conversing with some elderly folks outside the entrance to the church we visited in Kazan. These were the Christian believers that Nikita Khrushchev had said would eventually die out and be replaced by atheist Communists. There are still many Russian Orthodox Christians in Russia to this day. Communism is the feature of the Soviet Union that died out.

The geodesic dome that housed our exhibit in Kazan. Visible on the right is the Apollo 10 command module, which stood at the entrance to the facility.

The large Univac computer complex shown inside the exhibit dome in Kazan. Technicians of that era would be amazed to learn that now a handheld device is much more powerful than this behemoth.

Paved road outside Kazan, which we traveled to the youth camp. Notice the dwellings of that period.

An even more representative picture of the area near Kazan. This was "out in the boonies."

The original note (in Russian) passed to me by the little old man at the exhibit in Kazan. Quite risky for him to have done so, even at his age. Note: The English translation appears previously in the chapter.

A horse-drawn cart in Kazan. In 1972, this was still a viable option for people to transport goods to and from the outlying areas in remote regions of the country, such as Kazan.

This shows me flanked by two waiters in front of the Hotel Volga in Kazan. One of the staff spilled the beans as to what we had been eating when ordering "beef" at the restaurant.

VACATION NUMBER ONE

It would be so nice if something
would make sense for a change.
— from Disney's 1951 film adaptation
of Lewis Carroll's *Alice in Wonderland*

BACK THROUGH MOSCOW

As was the case after our exhibit closed in each city in which it was shown, our twenty guides split up into small groups and traveled to various parts of the USSR on "vacation." Our travel arrangements had to be submitted to our American supervisors for approval and also set up by the Soviet authorities who monitored and controlled our movements around the country.

Some of us decided to return to Moscow and from there travel to the Baltic republics of Estonia and Latvia and then to the Black Sea resort city of Sochi. It was the start of an eleven-day excursion that would cost each of us $375, with that price including all transportation, lodging, tours, and three meals a day.

This was my second stopover in Moscow. Here our group spent a couple of days relaxing, sleeping in, and again enjoying some American cuisine at the US embassy commissary. I took a few rides on the famous Moscow subway—an elaborate underground rail system constructed in the 1930s under the supervision of Nikita Khrushchev when he was a rising young star in the Soviet system. Escalators transported passengers from the upper areas of the central Moscow subway station down to the train areas below.

The most impressive part of the Moscow Metro system was the ornate design of some of the larger stations. I recall thinking to myself that I would have never dreamed of a subway station sporting so much marble and even chandeliers suspended from the high ceilings.

One humorous aspect of riding the Soviet subway in Moscow was the timing of the closing of the trains' doors. Prior to departing for the next stop, in the West one usually expects to hear an announcement such as "Next stop (such and such); Caution, the doors will be closing," followed within a few seconds by the pneumatic doors closing. Here, I know not why, the sequence was something like "Attention, comrades, the doors"—whereupon the doors suddenly slammed shut—"are closing." I suppose one was expected to know this, but I almost lost part of my shirt during this process. Just one more thing to learn about life in the Soviet Union.

This stopover in Moscow led to one of the most interesting and enlightening occurrences of my entire Soviet trip. One evening, a friend and I headed out to have dinner at the Hotel *Ukraina*—a famous landmark in Moscow. As we waited to be seated, we noticed a group of four black men also waiting for a table. They heard us speaking English and approached us, asking if we were perhaps Americans.

This struck up a conversation that led to our being seated with these gentlemen at a table in the hotel's large dining room. They turned out to be foreign exchange students from a small African nation. The leader of their group spoke very good Russian. This was his final year of study at Moscow State University. During dinner I asked him whether his country sent many of their exchange students to Moscow.

"Oh yes," he replied, "we send all of them here to the Soviet Union."

I found this somewhat curious, and followed up with him as to the reason.

"Well," he said, "we used to send quite a few of our students to Princeton, Columbia, and Berkeley, but they all came back Marxists. Now we send them here, and after three or four years in the USSR, they all return dedicated anti-Communists, and most remain so for the rest of their lives."

This was quite an indictment of America's higher-education system. The more I have observed our colleges and universities during the forty-five years since my time in the Soviet Union, the more I understand what the young African student meant.

The only other memorable thing I recall about this short stopover in Moscow is the ice cream. It was still summer, and the Russians made the best-tasting ice cream I'd ever had. The flavor was almost indescribable—thick, rich, and very creamy. Not exactly a health-conscious treat, but one I thoroughly enjoyed.

As this was but a brief stop in transit for us, we had little time for sightseeing. That would have to wait until our final stay in Moscow a couple of months later. Meanwhile, it was off to the Baltics for a few days of rest and relaxation.

TALLINN

Our first stay in the Baltics was in Tallinn—in those years the capital of the Estonian Soviet Socialist Republic, and now the capital of a free and independent nation. It is located on the northern coast of Estonia, on the shore of the Gulf of Finland. Like its other Baltic neighbors—Latvia and Lithuania—due to geography and geopolitical realities, Estonia has seen more than its fair share of war and has suffered the consequences of being invaded many times by Germany from the west and by the Soviet Union in the east.

Founded in the early thirteenth century, Tallinn is among the oldest capital cities of Northern Europe. Its "Old Town" is one of the finest representations of European medieval cities. I'm told it remains so to this day.

Tallinn was occupied by Kaiser Wilhelm II's German troops in 1917, then by Soviet troops in 1940, and again by Nazi troops in 1941. In 1944, it was "liberated" by the Red Army, although, as the Estonians were to find out in short order, this really wasn't liberation in the true sense of the word. Rather, it amounted to yet another military takeover by troops who would forcibly subjugate the people to tyranny and dictatorship, and it resulted in a one-way trip to the GULAG for thousands of Estonians.

Estonia, Latvia, and Lithuania would become independent nations after the fall of the Soviet Union. But that wouldn't come until 1992. These countries had been ceded to Stalin by the 1939 German-Soviet "nonaggression" pact, and Soviet troops took them over in 1940. This was followed by mass arrests and deportations of Latvians, Estonians, and Lithuanians. Stalin had a record of never trusting anyone who had even traveled to foreign countries, much less those who had actually lived in a free society.

We stayed in the Viru hotel—a newly built Intourist hotel. Completed in early 1972 by Finnish contractors, it was Tallinn's only high-rise building at that time. Many years later I learned that two years after the 1991 dissolution of the Soviet Union, it was discovered that the hotel's twenty-third floor had contained a KGB monitoring center where they operated and coordinated hidden espionage devices in the guest rooms, bar, and restaurant areas.

In that regard, foreigners staying in Tallinn were subjected to the same 24/7/365 surveillance as in every other area of the USSR. By this time in our journey, we had all become quite used to being followed everywhere and having our conversations constantly monitored. Every now and then, this stifling environment produced some very interesting and revealing moments. One occurred during a dinner in Tallin's Old Town, the historical part of the city that featured shops and restaurants with a local, ethnic flavor.

For dinner, at the recommendation of our tour guide, we chose an ethnic Estonian restaurant in Old Town. We were told to be ready for a long wait to be seated since this popular restaurant was always crowded. After entering, we sat in a waiting area for about forty-five minutes. We were finally seated at a table and then began the usual Soviet-style kabuki dining routine that I had first experienced in the Metropol Hotel in Moscow. After dropping off the menus and scurrying away, the waiters would reappear and hustle past our table with seemingly little regard for how long we had been sitting there. Suddenly I got the idea to switch from speaking Russian to speaking English among ourselves.

One waiter paused and listened intently to our conversation. He walked up to our table and asked in heavily accented English, "You are maybe British?"

I replied that we were Americans and showed him my passport. The next thing I knew, we were surrounded by what seemed like ten waiters and waitresses who immediately took our order and got it back to us in record time.

The Russians in the restaurant were virtually ignored from the moment this happened. They began shouting and cursing loudly in Russian about not having their orders taken—to no avail as the Estonian food servers simply ignored them. This seemed to me yet another refutation of the Soviet propaganda line about how thrilled all the peoples of the USSR were to be living in a Communist "paradise." Many Estonians seemed less than ecstatic at having been forcibly incorporated into Socialist Wonderland, and incidents such as this one in the restaurant appeared to bear that out.

After the Viru hotel was completed by Finnish contractors earlier in 1972, several of the Finns had been asked to remain on-site to assist the Soviets with any construction-related problems that might arise. This led to some interesting interactions in the hotel's bar.

The Finnish and Estonian languages are very similar.[1] Thus, Finns and Estonians can converse with each other with ease. I watched with amazement how the bartenders in the Viru's "currency bar" spoke openly with the visiting Finns.[2] One of the Finns translated for us, and I was surprised at how many anti-Soviet jokes were told to them by the Estonians. Perhaps they got

---

1. Along with Hungarian, Finnish and Estonian both belong to the Finno-Ugric language group.
2. Intourist hotels where foreigners were allowed to stay in the USSR had facilities where one could spend rubles or the currencies of their native countries.

away with this since they weren't speaking Russian, which made it more difficult for the KGB to eavesdrop.

It was clear to me that many if not most among the ethnic population of Tallinn treated the presence of Russians in their country as a genuine "occupation." I recently learned that that term is still used in Estonia to describe the Soviet era in that country—both prior to World War II and during 1944 through 1991.

Our vacation package included tours. Intourist took our group on a brief jaunt to the outskirts of Tallinn, where we saw, among other things, an impressive memorial to the horrors Estonia had experienced in World War II. As we would see many more times during our stay in the USSR, such monuments and war memorials were among the most frequently visited places on all sightseeing trips arranged for foreigners in the Soviet Union.

After two days in Tallinn, it was time to take our first train trip inside the USSR. This trip reminded me of train rides I had taken some years before in Germany. The compartments were comfortable, and we saw quite a bit of the Baltic countryside. Due to the short distance to Riga, we were actually allowed to take a day train. It would be our last opportunity to view the scenery during daylight hours. Our future train trips would all be made at night, as will be explained in later chapters.

RIGA

Our next vacation stop was in Riga, the capital at that time of the Latvian Soviet Socialist Republic and currently the capital of the independent country of Latvia. Located on the Gulf of Riga, it was, like Tallinn, founded in the early thirteenth century. And, as with Tallinn, Riga offered many interesting places to see and visit. We got to take a half-day trip into the countryside and saw examples of how the native Latvians lived in ancient times. Another similarity between Tallinn and Riga had to do with the relations between the local ethnic population and Soviet Russians. The residents of Riga seemed no more thrilled to be a part of the Soviet Union than the Estonians.

We stayed in a hotel near Riga's Old Town, on a street near the main thoroughfare through the city. After checking into our hotel and having breakfast, our small group wandered out for some sightseeing.

At a bus stop, we came upon an old man who was very surprised to see Russian-speaking Americans in his city. While waiting for the bus, he recounted to us an interesting irony about the street we were on. In 1972 this street was called "Lenin Street." He said that during the Nazi occupation of the 1940s, it had been called "Adolf Hitler Street." The man noted wryly that during Latvian independence before Soviet occupation and before the Germans renamed it, the street had been called "Freedom Street." That a street named in honor of freedom would later bear the names of Hitler and Lenin was indeed a bitter irony.

Shortly before our bus arrived, the old man noticed how one member of our group was looking at the top of the buildings across the street. In the Soviet era, it was customary for Communist Party slogans to be posted in huge letters atop high buildings. The letters were probably fifteen feet tall.[3] This little old fellow then also looked up and began reading aloud the words appearing in Russian atop these structures: "Peace, Unity, Brotherhood, Freedom, Joy." He then gave us a deadpan look and said, "Yep. All the things we don't have here."

Judging by his reaction to these slogans atop the buildings, I was pretty sure that this gentleman probably hadn't looked up there in twenty years. And why should he? The flowery words of the Soviet Government and party slogans had nothing whatsoever to do with the reality of life in Soviet Latvia.

We were also taken on a short day-trip into the Latvian countryside, where we did some sightseeing. The ethnic structures and memorial monuments were very similar to those we had seen in Tallinn. Nothing earthshaking occurred during

3. This was commonplace in most Soviet cities. Large banners often adorned the walls of big buildings, and Soviet slogans were visible atop such buildings in very large letters to ensure their visibility from the ground. There seemed to be no respite from Soviet propaganda.

our stay in Riga. It was just nice to be able to relax and not have to deal with Soviet plants agitating us as they had at the Kazan exhibit.

For a change of pace, we had scheduled our final leg of this trip to the Black Sea resort of Sochi. Since the distance was over 1,100 miles, we decided against a train trip, which would have taken almost three days to reach our destination. Instead, we again boarded an Ilyushin turboprop aircraft, and off we flew.

SOCHI

In this part of our journey, we traversed a large segment of the European portion of the USSR. The four-hour flight was, by Soviet standards of the time, uneventful. Of course, there were the usual moments that were rather uncomfortable for people used to the niceties of flying, say, Delta Air Lines back in the day. For example, I just couldn't get used to sitting in a cramped plane waiting forever on the tarmac for the aircraft's cabin to be pressurized and thus for the air to begin coming through the overhead vents. We had experienced this in Moscow, and it seemed to be a staple of all Aeroflot flights within the Soviet Union.

Some aspects of this flight, however, differed slightly from our previous air adventures. Instead of seeing an oily substance leaking from one of the engines, this time one of them began emitting a thin trail of smoke. I thought to myself, *Here we go again.*

And then there was the landing. During the 1960s and early 1970s, many if not most of the Aeroflot commercial pilots had been Soviet Air Force pilots during World War II. This apparently included a number of former dive-bomber pilots for whom the term "glide path" was just a nebulous concept. On virtually all commercial flights throughout the world, an aircraft approaching an airfield travels down a "glide path" that involves a gradual descent to the airfield. With many of these Soviet pilots, this did not seem to exist. As we approached the Sochi airfield, suddenly the plane began a very rapid descent, similar, I suppose, to the manner in which World War II dive bombers attacked their targets on the ground. This produced a quite uncomfortable sensation of being glued to the back of one's seat for much of the approach. Only as the airfield became visible did the pilot level off and decrease speed and altitude for his landing.

We had scheduled our trip from Sochi to Donetsk by air, but I was now determined that this would be the very last time I would board an Aeroflot aircraft. After flirting with possible disaster five times in just over two months, I decided that from Donetsk through the end of my time in the USSR, I would take the train.

Our time in Sochi was uneventful. We simply enjoyed the final couple of days away from the hustle and bustle of working the exhibit. Unlike today's Sochi, this resort area was rather small in 1972 and sported mainly a beach and a few minor sightseeing opportunities. About the only memorable occasion was when our small group was relaxing in the hotel and suddenly a funnel cloud appeared over the Black Sea. Everything became quite dark—a tornado, we feared. But, to our relief, the storm passed as suddenly as it had arrived.

ON TO DONETSK

Our first vacation in the USSR ended on September 3, at which time we flew from Sochi to Donetsk. Soon the routine would begin again and we would find ourselves immersed in work. Nonetheless, I reasoned, time would pass quicker that way. Several of us were already starting to count the days until we would get to go home.

The skyline of Tallinn in 1972. The tall white building in the middle is the Viru hotel—the only multistory building in Tallinn at the time. It was where our group stayed during our first "vacation."

Founded in the early thirteenth century, Tallinn is among the oldest capitals of Northern Europe. Its "Old Town" is one of the finest representations of European medieval cities. It remains a popular site for tourists visiting Estonia.

The Dome Church on Toompea Hill in Tallinn. Another part of antiquity spared destruction and maintained to this day as a historical site.

A view of the port of Tallinn from "Old Town." At the right is the ancient Church of the Holy Ghost.

The beautiful Russalka monument in Tallinn memorializes the 1893 loss at sea of a Russian naval vessel on its way to Finland. Here the angel is holding a Russian Orthodox cross.

A tour took us to several monuments in the Riga area. This shows Brothers' Cemetery, which honors the war dead.

This display atop a factory building in Riga is the type of propaganda that the old man with whom we had talked about Communist Party slogans had apparently been ignoring for decades. This one reads: "Turn the Decisions of the 24th Communist Party Congress into Reality!"

More examples of slogans that appeared throughout the Soviet Union in the 1970s. The one at the top of this building reads: "Glory to the Soviet People." The red sign reads: "Long Live the Union of Soviet Socialist Republics." These serve as evidence of the constant barrage of Soviet propaganda to which the people were exposed every day.

Our hotel in Sochi. Very luxurious accommodations compared to Kazan. Such hotels as this were among the finest that Intourist had to offer and attracted many visitors to this area.

View of the Black Sea from our hotel in Sochi.

One of the frequent summer storms, which seemed to arise without warning over the Black Sea. When we saw this one through the dining room window of our hotel in Sochi, we were a bit concerned. Fortunately, as the darkness blew over, this storm passed as instantly as it had arisen. Anyone who hasn't witnessed one of these cannot fully appreciate the ferocity of the high winds and the darkness that suddenly descends on the area. Never having been this close to one of these, I won't ever forget the experience.

I photographed this view of the Sochi railway terminal on our ride in from the airport. As the buses in the foreground show, Sochi was a mecca for tourists during this era. It remains so to this day, thanks in part to the Black Sea beaches and to the huge investment the Russians have made to expand Sochi's facilities.

DONETSK

Imagine the Titanic sinking every day for thirteen years!
Such were the losses from the
1933 Famine Genocide in Soviet Ukraine.
— Melanie Bobrowski

ARRIVAL IN DONETSK

In early September, our first rest and relaxation time had come to an end. We reported to our next exhibit city—Donetsk—located in the coal-rich Donbas region of what was then the Ukrainian Soviet Socialist Republic. This was the eastern Ukraine—an area that, due to its industrial importance and for political reasons, had been "Russianized" in the 1930s.[1]

Our training in Washington had focused on statistics of the American coal industry since questions about that were sure to arise in Donetsk, with so many of the visitors who would attend our exhibit there being connected with the mining industry. Unfortunately, there was one historical fact on which we were not briefed concerning the eastern Ukraine: the *Holodomor*, the Ukrainian word for "genocide by starvation."[2] Any discussion of Donetsk, given its geographical location, needs to include a brief description of this matter.

In the early 1930s, Soviet dictator Josef Stalin had launched his plan to forcibly collectivize Soviet agriculture. The Ukraine

---

1. As Ukrainians were deported to labor camps and others starved to death, the Soviets reportedly sent ethnic Russians into the Ukraine to take their place.
2. For in-depth details of this horrendous event, consult the book *The Harvest of Sorrow* listed in the bibliography.

is a highly productive agricultural area, so it was especially hard-hit by this measure. Stalin's secret police were ordered to travel across the entire Ukraine and confiscate grain that Ukrainian peasants were rumored to have hidden in their efforts at resisting the collectivization of all agriculture.

What resulted was the intentional, forced starvation of seven to eight million Ukrainians, many of them in the eastern regions. This left a scar on that part of the country, which is still evident to this day in the now independent Ukraine. According to official Soviet records, in 1933 alone, over a thousand family members of collective and private farmers engaged in industrial production in the Donbas region were "taken off the supply list." Translation: They were deprived of food.

As an aside, the area in and around Donetsk remains a cauldron of ethnic friction and hostility between Ukrainians and Russian "separatists" who want the area annexed into the Russian Federation.

On one of my first walks around Donetsk, I noticed that several of the signs in the city were in the Ukrainian language. Although similar to Russian, this is a distinctly separate East Slavic language. So, I decided to see if I could find a Ukrainian-Russian, Russian-Ukrainian dictionary. I went to a local bookstore and asked the fellow working there if he had this dictionary. He gave me a puzzled look and said, "What kind of dictionary? We have no such book. Who would want one?"

The Soviet Union consisted of fifteen so-called republics, fourteen of which had a population whose ethnic heritage differed from that of Russia, especially as to languages. The only officially recognized language in the USSR was Russian, and everything—press, radio, TV, and all official business—was conducted in Russian. The Soviet Government viewed the use of any other language as being potentially detrimental to the unity and "socialist harmony" of the country. They applied this standard most stringently to Ukrainian. Later in my trip, in other parts of the Ukraine, I was to discover examples of this phenomenon. In Donetsk, although there were signs in Ukrainian, I heard only Russian spoken.

Our hotel accommodations were nicer here than we had experienced in Kazan. No trains waking us up in the middle of the night and no adjacent river with the accompanying bugs. The weather was a lot cooler as it was now fall—a very pleasant time of the year in that part of the world.

The hotel was located on one of the main streets of the city. My notes from the period reflect that there was a movie theater across the street, and I recall going there a couple of times during our stay. It was a small theater—and bare bones in comparison to American movie cinemas.

One movie stands out in my memory. It was a war movie depicting a fictional conflict in the Far East. This film was yet another example of the Soviet propaganda machine's constant drumbeat as to what I have referred to as 1970s' CDS (China Dread Syndrome). The plot of the movie centered on fictional combat in a far eastern region of the USSR. Border skirmishes were shown in some detail, and the "enemy" forces all had a distinctly Asian look.[3] The heroic Soviet military prevailed in the combat scenes shown on the screen. This latent fear of everything Chinese in 1972 seemed to permeate every area of the Soviet Union and appeared to cause considerable consternation among the citizenry. The message seemed clear: be prepared to defend your motherland yet again—this time against possible invasion from the east.

As an aside, amazing as it may seem, there were also jokes concerning this matter. One anecdote told of a (fictional) war having broken out between the Soviet Union and China. On the first day of this war, the Soviets took a million Chinese soldiers prisoner. Another million were captured on the second day and again on the third day. On the morning of the fourth day, Chinese leader Mao Tse-tung called Soviet Premier Leonid Brezhnev and asked, "Had enough?"

There really wasn't much to see in the way of sightseeing in Donetsk. The only tour the Soviets arranged for us during our time there was a day trip to a coal mine on the outskirts of the

---

3. During this time period, there had, in fact, been many border skirmishes on the Ussuri River, which formed the border between the USSR and China.

city. As one of the pictures at the end of this chapter suggests, this mine appeared to be rather primitive. I didn't ask, but I imagined that more than a few accidents may well have occurred at this facility over the years. I politely declined an invitation to go down into the shaft. Being somewhat claustrophobic, I had no desire to view the bowels of the mine. I decided to take the Soviets' word for it being a productive facility.

WORKING THE EXHIBIT IN DONETSK

After the usual set-up period, the exhibit opened on September 14. We quickly settled into our normal routine, including my again being assigned to work the Univac computer display with yet another German technician the company had sent.[4]

As predicted, many of the questions asked by the visitors in Donetsk had to do with the coal mining industry in the United States. And then there were questions about the societal issues, which closely resembled those we had been asked in Kazan, and hundreds of questions about life in America, including quite a few about the products we had on display.

But there was also the eternal laundry list of provocations via inquiries about the "oppressed" life in the United States. They were posed by a fresh set of local area plants. By this time in our journey, many of us were tiring of the constant rehashing of American social problems, about which these plants droned on and on. How many times can one continue to answer questions such as those below?

"Explain the American phenomenon of 'unemployment.' We have no such problem here."

"Why do your students have to pay for college? University education is provided free of charge here to all students."

"What is this thing called racism in your country? We are all equal here."

"Why do your citizens have to pay to go to the doctor? We are

---

4. The Univac corporation sent a different technician from their West German affiliate to each of our three exhibit cities. Apparently they reasoned that about a month in the USSR was enough for any of their employees to endure.

guaranteed free medical treatment, including hospitalization and medications."

"Is it true that your soldiers kill Vietnamese babies in your imperialist war?"

And on and on it went. Every conceivable social problem or issue imaginable was discussed ad nauseam and, I would add, nitpicked to death. These plants were indeed well trained and quite aggressive in describing every way that life in America (according to them) fell short of the utopia their government claimed existed in the Soviet Union.

Although we had been trained to avoid demeaning the USSR in discussing controversial issues, by this time in our Soviet journey, aside from being turned off by such discussions, many of us had developed some quite deft and often humorous ways of deflecting the provocative questions and diatribes of the plants.

For example, as to the moth-eaten question dealing with unemployment in America, one guide repeated in Donetsk the answer he had given in Kazan that he was not surprised that there was no unemployment in the Soviet Union since half the people were busy watching the other half. As it had in Kazan, this remark drew knowing smirks from the visitors who understood that it rebutted overt Soviet propaganda. The visitors clearly got the punch line of this story.

On another occasion, in answer to the intentionally provocative question about "free" Soviet health care, one guide answered with a joke he had heard from someone in Great Britain: "If you think your health care is expensive, just wait until it's free." This answer definitely struck a chord among the visitors in the crowd since they were only too aware of the hypocritical nature of this matter in the USSR. It was commonly known during this era that if one of your relatives had to be hospitalized, you'd better get to the doctors treating him or her and come up with some cash "on the side," as they put it, or some other enticement for your relative to get decent care.

As to the issue of "free education" in the USSR, I thought back to the discussion we had had with the African exchange students in Moscow and to their attitude about education and life in the Soviet Union. I decided not to bring this up in this forum since I didn't want to inadvertently cause any problems for those students, whom the secret police could have easily tracked down.

Additionally, as everyone in the country knew, the educational options for Soviet students were limited to the subject areas leading to professions that the state had preordained for them. And, rather than seeking a job after graduation, Soviets were assigned to a job in a location decided by the government. How "free" and wonderful, then, was such an educational system?

Just after noon one day, our German computer technician told me he had a throbbing toothache. I got permission to shut down the Univac stand for the afternoon and accompanied the tech to a dental clinic not far from our facility. This clinic apparently was a "standard" medical facility (i.e., the kind where run-of-the-mill Soviet citizens received treatment, as opposed to the special clinics where Communist Party members and Soviet officials went). Nothing fancy here. Just sort of a run-down building that more closely resembled a small manufacturing facility than a medical clinic.

It was here that our German friend got a taste of Soviet "free medical care." The dental technicians wired him up to some gadget, and they performed what I suppose was some sort of root canal. After thirty minutes of this torture, the German tech announced that his tooth felt "much better," and we headed back to our hotel. He later told me that he preferred enduring the pain for another couple of weeks to staying one more minute hooked up to that "hideous apparatus"—his words.

From time to time, the subject of the press and freedom of speech arose at our exhibit. I recall an incident that was very revealing about how most Soviet citizens simply accepted the stifling and often self-contradictory propaganda they endured every day. One morning, rather than having breakfast in our hotel, I decided to walk a couple of blocks down the street and eat at a place known as the miners' dining hall. It was frequented by coal miners on their way to work.

Prior to heading out to this facility, I grabbed a copy of

Pravda—the official newspaper of the Communist Party of the Soviet Union—and began reading it on my way to the dining hall. In bold headlines I read: "Another Record Harvest Achieved." The lead article claimed that Soviet agriculture had once again broken all previous records in grain production.

At the dining hall, after paying for my breakfast and grabbing a tray, I started through the line. There didn't seem to be much for the miners to choose from for their breakfast. Reaching the area where the bread was put out, I noticed that there were only a few pieces of what looked like rather stale bread. Above the bread bin was a large sign that read, translated from Russian: "Take only the bread you need; Bread is a treasure—conserve it."

None of the miners even glanced at the sign. They probably hadn't read the *Pravda* article, either. This contradiction between Soviet propaganda and daily life in the USSR seemed nonexistent to them. This reminded me of the old fellow in Riga who probably hadn't looked up at the Communist Party slogans atop the buildings in decades.

There was one strange feature that I had noticed at our exhibit. Quite a few coal miners would apparently come directly from work to our pavilion. The first time I saw some of them, I noticed that something seemed amiss. Their eyelashes were black, almost as if they were wearing mascara. I subsequently learned that this was coal dust, which accumulated around the miners' eyes at work. Apparently their masks were not of the quality of those worn in the West.

An interesting "issue" came up at the exhibit in Donetsk. It produced questions about why the American government was persecuting poor Angela Davis. Was it just for being a Communist?[5]

Shortly before our arrival in Donetsk, the Soviet Union had hosted a visit by then-member of the Communist Party of the USA Angela Davis. The Soviets spared no expense in rolling out

---

5. American Communist Party member Angela Davis had been charged with murder for links to Black Panther terrorists, but was acquitted on June 4, 1972, by a jury that held that the prosecution had failed to make its case as to her legal culpability in the murder.

the red carpet (no pun intended) for Davis during her trip. She (in)famously made a statement to the effect that she had never known what freedom was until she came to the Soviet Union. When asked about this matter by one rather obnoxious Soviet fellow at the exhibit, I replied, "Well, I can sort of relate to that since I never fully *appreciated* my freedom until I came to the Soviet Union." Not exactly the response the guy was trying to elicit. Many in the crowd beamed their approval, to the chagrin of the plants around the Univac stand that day.

And so the daily grilling continued. After a couple of hours of this torture inflicted by another plant dealing with every American social problem imaginable, as my one-hour break began, I retreated for a breather to an area behind the Univac stand. I poured myself a shot of Smirnov (American distilled) vodka, and screwed the plastic cap back on the bottle.

A little old man who observed me doing this peeked his head around the screen and asked if he could see the bottle. I handed it to him, at which time he unscrewed the plastic cap and then screwed it back on. He repeated this several times, then held up the plastic cap and asked, "What's this for?"

I told him it was to close the bottle.

"Close the bottle?" he asked in total bemusement.

I asked him what he did after taking a few drinks.

He quickly replied, "I throw away that bottle and go get another one."

Since Soviet alcohol bottles were sealed only with a thin tinfoil flange, the idea of resealing a bottle of vodka was indeed a culture shock for this guy who had quite a time understanding the concept of a resealable bottle of vodka. This was yet another indication of the drinking habits of many people in the old Soviet Union.

On the subject of alcohol consumption, during our stay in Donetsk the Soviet Government launched one of its frequent campaigns to combat alcoholism. Vodka was typically sold in so-called *gastronomy*—grocery and provisions shops. Many Soviet workers would stop every day at these places on their way home from work. The government decided to jam a broomstick in the spokes of their bicycles, as it were, by shutting off vodka sales at three thirty every afternoon.

And so, the vodka display counters were covered with large white sheets at three thirty. This, it was thought, would drastically reduce the availability of and thus the consumption of vodka. However, Soviet Russians could be quite inventive in responding to threats to their drinking habits. Thus, when confronted with this seemingly foolproof program, many Soviet workers simply left work early to make sure they could get to the *gastronom* before the sheets were brought out.

This was an example of the old saying "Where there's a will, there's a way." Instead of reducing alcohol consumption, this "campaign" likely only exacerbated the problem of absenteeism at Soviet factories as workers left early to get their daily vodka fix.

Another amusing and at the same time revealing incident happened toward the end of the exhibit in Donetsk. As I had done in Kazan, I managed to escape the Univac stand for an hour here and there to work the cars. Since only about one in fifty Soviet citizens in 1972 owned a vehicle, the three American automobiles we had on display stole the show at our exhibits.

As I was nearing an hour of answering questions about the cars, a fellow asked how much the Lincoln Continental cost. I told him the approximate price, and he produced his savings account book and offered to pay cash for it on the spot.[6] I replied that our cars were not for sale at the exhibit and added, as an aside, that very few people in the United States paid cash for their automobiles, opting instead to make a "down payment" and finance the vehicle on credit.

Well, this discussion of credit was a bridge too far for the fellow. Regardless of repeated attempts at explaining the concept to him, it was fruitless. Finally, another Soviet visitor tapped him on the shoulder and said, "Look, here we stand in line to buy cars;

---

6. In the USSR, one had to save up enough money to purchase a car. Only then could they place an order and get in line to have their car produced and delivered. It took years to save up such a sum, and then they had to wait another twelve to eighteen months to actually receive the vehicle.

in America the cars stand in line waiting to be purchased." The fellow just shook his head in disbelief and walked away.

Two things occurred in the late summer and in the fall of 1972, both of which had a discernable impact on the psyche of many Soviets. Russians love the game of chess, and it is one of their longstanding national pastimes. They take great pride in the success of their chess grandmasters, and thus it was quite a shock for them when young American upstart Bobby Fischer beat Soviet national chess champion Boris Spassky in a match in August.

Many Soviets at the exhibit, while acknowledging that Fischer was indeed a very talented chess player, nevertheless added comments such as "But he sure is an immature jerk." This loss had clearly stung them.

The second such demoralizing defeat occurred when the Canadian national hockey team defeated the Soviet national squad in an unprecedented game eight of the 1972 international championship match. As we watched on Soviet television in our hotel, the Canadians scored the winning goal with thirty-four seconds remaining. We smiled as the Canadians attending the game began chanting: "Da, da, Canada. Nyet, nyet Soviet." The Soviets really took this defeat hard, and their TV announcers immediately started denigrating the tough, physical style of play the Canadians had employed. I remember them saying things like "The Canadians don't play hockey. They're boxing!" Another remarked, "This isn't sports—it's street fighting!"

Not being an enthusiast of either chess or hockey, I did not gloat over these events. But there were instances at the exhibit when some of our guides, when coming under constant pounding by plants of how superior the Soviet system was in comparison to the that of the West, used these two stinging Russian defeats to get under their skin. It seemed to work pretty well.

And then there was one sad but telling incident in Donetsk. During a break in the action, I was having a cigarette outside the exhibit hall when a man approached me and, looking around to see if there were any policemen nearby, whispered to me, "I just want you to know that my wife and I would really like to invite you and some of your friends over to our apartment for dinner." And then, looking around again, he said, "But, well, you know . . ."

He didn't need to amplify. I understood full well what he meant. Were he to have invited me and had I been able to go have dinner at their place, as soon as I left, there would be a knock at the door and the secret police would start harassing them as to why they were meeting with an American. Was there some nefarious reason for it? Were they perhaps spies secretly working for the Americans? Or were they providing us anti-Soviet propaganda we might use? In Soviet Wonderland, even a simple act of hospitality or kindness shown to an American might be viewed by the authorities as an anti-Soviet activity.

How sad, I thought. Russians have long been known for their hospitality as a people. But this admirable human characteristic had to be suppressed in the USSR, lest it lead to negative and even dangerous consequences for the person exhibiting it.

One very interesting phenomenon was in evidence throughout our time in Donetsk. As previously mentioned, 1972 was an American election year pitting Democrat challenger George McGovern against the incumbent Republican president, Richard Nixon. At this time of the year, the election campaign was heating up, and it was a frequent topic of conversation at our exhibit.

What seemed to puzzle many Soviet visitors was the overt support shown by many of the guides for one candidate or another. They knew that we, as part of a US government cultural exchange exhibit, were working for the American government. We could tell them endlessly about freedom of speech and expression in the United States, but seeing open political statements in the form of election campaign buttons on our lapels was living proof of the concept.[7] Many were simply unable

---

7. Such activities on the part of federal employees were usually viewed as violations of the Hatch Act. But the USIA apparently had cleared this with someone in a position of authority since it did show freedom of speech versus the overt suppression of the same in the USSR. Besides, we were just temporary employees, not careerists.

to comprehend it, and I believe this made a lasting impression on them.

During our time in Donetsk, we had a visit from a well-known journalist and scholar of the time—William F. Buckley. Buckley was famous for being a staunch adversary of the Soviet Union. His writings lambasted Communism in general and the USSR in particular, so I was a bit surprised that the Soviets would let him travel there in 1972. I enjoyed meeting him and being able to converse with him about the USSR.

Our staff hosted a dinner for Buckley, which was attended by some of the Soviet Chamber of Commerce and Intourist people. One of my fellow guides was assigned to translate for Buckley at the dinner, and he relayed one interesting moment from the evening. Buckley was asked by one of the attendees what he thought the future held for the Soviet Union. Buckley gave the man a wry look and simply said, "It's imperiled." It took twenty years to come about, but he turned out to be right in the end.

Buckley wrote up his experience in Donetsk in an article entitled "Boring from Within the USSR" in which he described the USIA exhibit program in general and our exhibit in particular.[8]

In his article, Buckley described some of the details of our exhibit, including the fact that it was staffed by "a couple of dozen young Americans who act not only as guides, but as seminar leaders" and who were "necessarily fluent in Russian." He quoted one of our folks as telling him that "one of the guys came here left of Mao Tse-tung" and "after three months in Russia, he's to the right of George Wallace."

Buckley also wrote that "several of the guides wear McGovern buttons on their lapels" and that this stunned the Soviet visitors to the exhibit. He quoted one member of our group as telling him that "many of the Russian visitors come back, some as many as a dozen times," ostensibly, as Buckley surmised, to see "whether the young bearded guide with the McGovern button had been vaporized and replaced with a Sears,

8. The article was published in late 1972 by the *Washington Star-News Syndicate*.

Roebuck Nixonite." Buckley concluded his article by noting that since this had not happened, the Russians were stunned.

HEADING OUT FOR ANOTHER VACATION

The exhibit closed in Donetsk on October 15, and the process of loading it up began. This gave me another opportunity to talk to some "old timers" among the Soviet laborers and collect a few more jokes and interesting insights on the USSR from folks who had been born and raised there. Soon we would be off to Odessa on the Black Sea to begin our second vacation trip.

Donetsk had provided some revealing moments, and our stay there helped confirm several aspects of life in the USSR, especially regarding its economy, lack of any semblance of freedom of the press, and working conditions of people such as the coal miners. As had been the case in Kazan, many of the conversations at the exhibit in Donetsk had provided me with genuine insights into what Soviet citizens of that era had to deal with.

William F. Buckley was right in his claim of the benefit of direct dialogue with Soviet visitors to American cultural exchange exhibits. The regular Ivan Ivanovich got to converse with real Americans in the flesh and in his native language. The guides were able to share the story of the United States with these regular Soviet citizens despite the ever-present plants and other stooges sent there to disrupt these interactions. We were also greatly benefitted by this opportunity to enhance our Russian-language skills in what is known as a total immersion environment.

As I think back on my time in Donetsk, another quote from *Alice in Wonderland* comes to mind: "I can't go back to yesterday because I was a different person then."

Our exhibit pavilion in Donetsk. This was a rather large sports arena—quite sufficient to house the dozens of items we put on display and to accommodate the thousands of visitors who would come to see our show and talk with us.

Large containers ready for unpacking and transfer into the exhibit pavilion. It was in these large containers that our exhibit items made the journey to and from each city in which it was shown.

During our excursion to the coal mine near Donetsk, I managed to take advantage of our tour guide's lack of attention just long enough to snap this picture of a Soviet military facility as we drove by. The sign reads "Glory to the Heroic Armed Forces of the USSR." I'm glad I was not seen shooting this picture. Even such an innocuous photograph of what I'm sure was a very minor military facility could have landed me in hot water. The Soviets were extremely sensitive to everything related to their military.

The coal mine near Donetsk that we visited during our approved tour of the area. In 1972 this facility was already quite old and would have never passed safety inspections in the West. Notice the picture of Vladimir Lenin symbolically supervising the work at the mine.

Soviet workers saw signs such as this one at virtually every work site. The slogan on the columns reads "Glory to Labor." Indeed.

VACATION NUMBER TWO

They died on the very edge of Europe.
And Europe didn't even notice it.
The world didn't even notice it—6 million persons!
—Aleksandr Solzhenitsyn, on the famine in the Ukraine
(1932–33)

B y the time the exhibit closed in Donetsk and we had packed it up for transport to Leningrad, we were very ready to head out on our second vacation excursion. We had become "veterans" of time spent in the USSR, and for many of us at least, our attitudes had hardened as to dealing with the daily routine of surveillance, moth-eaten anti-American slogans, and incessant propaganda depicting the United States as the bogeyman of the world and the source of all human evil.

And so, with a bit thicker skin and in need of some rest and relaxation time, a small group of us headed out to see some different areas of the Ukraine—then the Ukrainian Soviet Socialist Republic—while our exhibit rode the rails to Leningrad.

The places we would visit during this time had suffered immensely—both during Stalin's reign of terror in the 1930s and at the hands of Nazi German invaders in the 1940s. The scars of those times were still evident in the Ukraine of 1972. The fear and paranoia caused by Stalin's Great Terror continued to lurk just beneath the surface of people's interactions with one another. The physical reconstruction of the infrastructure of many of the cities from the damage of the war had still not been completed. And many of the people still bore the physical and emotional scars caused by seeing so much destruction.

ODESSA

Our first stop on this vacation was the Black Sea port of Odessa. The night train involved a very long overnight ride. As usual when traveling by train, especially during the night, we weren't able to view anything from our compartments. We didn't arrive in Odessa until late in the afternoon of the following day. The weather for our brief stay here was very comfortable—in the low sixties range, as I recall.

The city was founded in 1794. In the 1970s, it was a primary commercial port and naval base. In 1941, the city was besieged and thereafter occupied by Romanian forces allied with Nazi Germany. The city was badly damaged during the war and during its recapture by the Red Army in 1944.

One of the main sightseeing attractions in Odessa is the Potemkin Stairs—a large stairway leading from the port into the city. It is 155 yards from top to bottom and is unique in that it creates an optical illusion. The view from the top seems to show no steps, only landings. From below, only the steps are visible.[1] In 1972, a long escalator aside the staircase provided a comfortable way to get to the top. We had walked down the staircase to get to the port. However, as to getting back to the top, I rode the escalator since 155 yards is a long hike up the steep incline. The staircase was immortalized in a famous 1925 Soviet movie, *Battleship Potemkin*, glorifying a 1905 workers' revolt.

At the well-known Londonskaya Hotel in Odessa, we experienced another very Soviet dining event. Two of us were having lunch there and had just completed our thirty-minute menu ordeal of ordering and reordering until we stumbled onto a dish they actually had. At the other end of the spacious dining hall sat a group of British tourists waiting for their meals. I noticed waiters carrying the Brits their food and happened to see *pompushki*[2] on some of the trays. I hailed our waitress and asked if

---

1. See the photos at the end of this chapter for views from both the top and bottom of this huge staircase.
2. *Pompushki* are delicious Ukrainian garlic-filled bread rolls baked and served with butter.

we could get some of those, too. She exploded and screamed very loudly, "Those aren't for you! Pay attention to your own dish!"

We visited the Odessa Theatre of Opera and Ballet for a performance. This very old building escaped damage during the war and was still a beautiful facility at the time of our visit. A little culture never hurts, and I enjoyed the evening.

After a day of uneventful, routine sightseeing around the Primorsky Bulvar area, where our hotel was located, we boarded a night train for the relatively short rail trip (275 miles) to Kiev, where our second vacation trip would continue.

KIEV

Our next stop was the ancient city of Kiev. Founded in the late ninth century, it is one of the oldest cities in Europe. In 1972 it was the capital of the Ukrainian Soviet Socialist Republic and is currently the capital of the independent country of Ukraine.

Kiev was the center of the East Slavic civilization known as Kievan *Rus*. It is the place where, in the year 988, Saint Vladimir baptized the Kievans into the Eastern Orthodox Christian faith, which remains today the largest religion in Russia. Vladimir's statue stands high on the hills overlooking the city.

The Great Famine of the early 1930s touched Kiev as it did virtually the entire Ukraine. The Kievan intelligentsia was almost completely eliminated in Stalin's purge of the middle and late 1930s. In World War II, the city suffered massive damage and was occupied by German troops for two years. Many atrocities took place there, including the murder of some one hundred thousand people in a nearby area known as Babi Yar. In short, Kiev suffered extensively during the Soviet era.

Our first day here was taken up by sightseeing. We began by boarding a bus on *Khreshchatik*—the main street running through downtown Kiev. It was during this bus ride that I got my second peek behind the curtain at the rigid enforcement of Russian as the only language that was to be used throughout the USSR.

After taking our seats on the bus, I noticed a man and his young son seated across from us. As we drove through the city, the boy asked his father a question in Ukrainian. The father interrupted him, pressed his finger to his lips, and asked the boy in Russian: "Where are we?" The young lad got the point right away and switched to Russian. This was a sign that, while the use of Ukrainian might have been okay at home, it was to be avoided in public, lest it attract the attention of the enforcers of the one-language rule.

It was yet another indication of the blunt force with which the Soviet Government, through its Russian-led majority, tamped down any sense of ethnic pride or cultural heritage. They weren't about to let "old ways" get in the way of the eternal building of a Communist paradise. No ethnic opposition—including speaking a language other than Russian—was to be tolerated in this monolithic state.

During our stay in Kiev, we visited the famous *Pecherska Lavra*—the Cave Monastery. This treasure of Eastern Orthodoxy was founded as a monastery in the mid-eleventh century, and its complex of churches has long been a historical preserve of East Slavic culture. Underneath one of the churches is a "cave" beneath which lie the remains of several of the most widely known saints of the Eastern Orthodox Church.

During the Soviet era, the bodies of the saints lying in repose were left uncovered as a sign of disrespect of religion by the Communist government. Many years after our visit, I learned that after the collapse of the Soviet Union, each of the bodies of these revered figures of Russian church history was covered with a cloth out of respect.

We spent our last evening in Kiev at the Philharmonic Hall attending a symphony conducted by the renowned Soviet Armenian composer and conductor Aram Khachaturian. I cannot now recall through the years how our chance meeting with him occurred, but I distinctly remember his inviting three of us to his suite for a glass of wine, where he graciously autographed our programs of the evening.[3] As I recall, he was

---

3. A photo reproduction of this program appears in the picture section at the end of this chapter. While it is written in Ukrainian, once again the only language heard at this event was Russian.

very glad to have met three Russian-speaking Americans and treated us very cordially.

BACK TO MOSCOW ONE LAST TIME

On October 29, we boarded a night train from Kiev to Moscow to spend a couple of days in the capital before heading to our final exhibit city, Leningrad. As usual, we had to take a night train since the Soviets didn't want us accidently catching sight of anything that could be remotely construed as "secret" information.

As I recall, the train pulled out of the railway station in Kiev for the 470-mile journey to Moscow somewhere around 7:00 p.m. This train had a small "buffet," which was actually nothing more than a tiny compartment from which they sold snacks and liquor. Interestingly, just behind the guy working in the buffet was a wooden case. When I asked the attendant what was in the box, he moved aside and I could read the words "Pilsner Urquell" on the case.

Ecstatic, I motioned to my fellow travelers from the group to quickly come up with whatever the cost of the beer would be. It was Czech beer—one of the best I had ever tasted in Germany during my military tour of duty there. I told the fellow in the buffet that we'd take the beer.

He asked, "How many bottles do you want?"

I quickly replied, "We'll take the whole case."

Somewhat astonished at this, he nevertheless put the case onto the serving shelf, whereupon we quickly paid him and whisked the entire case off to our compartment.

This proved to be the most enjoyable and relaxing of all my travels around the USSR. The three of us guzzled down the beer in about an hour and slept the rest of the way to Moscow. As usual, there was nothing we could view during the nighttime ride anyway. The train pulled into the station in Moscow early the next morning.

During our third and final brief stayover there, I took time to do the routine, perfunctory sightseeing that most tourists do in

Moscow, such as walking along the banks of the Moscow River, photographing the Kremlin, riding the Moscow subway system, etc. There was one stop on my itinerary, however, that differed somewhat as to how most tourists do things.

I decided to make the obligatory jaunt to the Lenin Mausoleum on Red Square and chose for my visit the date of October 31, in honor of a great holiday: Halloween. One American embassy employee joked that this would be a very appropriate time to go to the "wax works" and view the remains of the ghoul whom he mockingly referred to as the "peasant under glass."[4] Such statements were best made only in the safe zone of foreign embassies in Moscow, as any such reference to Vladimir Lenin—the founder and glorious hero of the Soviet Union—could actually be criminally prosecuted as "slander" against the Soviet Union and its leadership.

Visiting this quasi-holy site of Communism is truly an eerie experience. While approaching the mausoleum from Red Square, one first notices the armed military guards posted at the entrance to the building. They, along with a number of uniformed policemen inside the edifice, maintain a stern, piercing stare as they scan every visitor during the entire time one is inside the dark, foreboding building. Hats were ordered removed out of reverence.

And then there was the graveyard-like silence. Even children accompanied by their parents uttered not one sound—no questions, no comments, not even a cough or a sneeze. This, coupled with the utter darkness of the place, produced a feeling of being in a haunted house at midnight.

Upon entering the structure, one descends a staircase that winds around the glass coffin in which Lenin's remains lie. The distance between this stairway and the coffin itself prevents a "close-up" view of the body. After winding in a semicircle around the coffin, the stairway then ascends back up to an exit, where I suddenly found myself in the bright sunlight of Red Square,

---

4. Lenin's embalmed remains are encased in a glass coffin on display at the mausoleum. Only his head and hands are visible. It has a waxen appearance, leading to the satirical reference to the Lenin Mausoleum as the "wax works."

thinking how appropriate it was to have taken this macabre pilgrimage to Lenin's eternal, dungeon-like resting place on Halloween.

I took advantage of this brief stay in Moscow to catch an opera at the Bolshoi Theatre—*Swan Lake*, as I recall. A couple of us also walked past KGB headquarters—the infamous Lubyanka. In this imposing building, Stalin's secret-police interrogators had tortured thousands of victims of the purges and terror of the 1930s and 1940s. I thought as I passed by how horrible it must have been to be transported to this brutal place, knowing that a concentration camp was the next (and, for many, the last) step in a person's journey through life.

For obvious reasons, we decided to view it from across the street and take no pictures of it, just in case. In that regard, I suppose some of us had begun to think as Soviet citizens did. No good could come from poking a bear with a stick. Just look down and go on your way.

In addition to again taking rides on the Moscow subway, I also went on walks to places such as Gorky Park. There I stopped to get a drink of carbonated soda water that was sold through dispensing machines. Immediately I noticed that there was only one "communal" glass, from which everyone drank. Not the most hygienic way to serve beverages.

Suddenly a Soviet fellow, after depositing his five-kopeck piece and pressing the button to release the soda, starting banging on the dispenser and shouted, "These accursed things are just like Soviet savings banks. You put money in but never get anything out!" I decided to forego the soda water and continued on my walk.

As I had done on previous occasions, as often as possible I headed for the commissary in the American embassy to enjoy food that reminded me of home. It would be the last such opportunity to enjoy familiar menus until we arrived in Helsinki, Finland a few weeks later.

One day, two of us managed to hitch a ride to a "foreign currency store" with a driver from the American embassy.[5] When we arrived, the driver parked the car, and before heading into the store with us, he took out a screwdriver and removed the windshield wipers. I asked why he was doing that, and he pointed out that even in Moscow spare auto parts were in high demand. So, he explained, if we were to leave them on the car and go into the store, it was guaranteed that they would be gone when we returned. In a society such as the old Soviet Union, supply of consumer goods could never keep up with demand. Therefore, theft was rampant and a black market for a host of goods flourished.

During our ride back to the embassy, we had stopped, waiting to turn left at an intersection, when a car drove up next to us. The driver was speeding through traffic and apparently didn't see a little old guy crossing the street in front of him. I remember thinking that the pedestrian was going to get run over by this fellow. Luckily, the driver hit the brakes and stopped about two feet short of hitting the pedestrian. The driver rolled down the window, leaned out, and in typical Soviet fashion yelled at him, "What, are you tired of living, grandpa?" and sped off. I think I heard more screaming in the USSR than I did during my eight-week Army basic training at Fort Dix, New Jersey, in 1966.

Our embassy friend also drove us past a place with no windows, no signs, but a heavy wooden door. He stopped across the street, pointed to this building and asked whether we knew what it was. We obviously didn't, so he explained that this was a "special store" for members of the Communist Party. One would never know it from the exterior appearance, but this was one of several exclusive stores in Moscow not open to the general public.

It was at such special stores in Soviet cities that loyal party members could purchase products not available in regular Soviet stores—goods such as top-shelf vodka, black caviar, meat from Finland, and beer from Germany. Loyalty to the Communist Party on the part of its apparatchiks was duly rewarded in Leonid Brezhnev's Soviet Union of the 1970s.

---

5. Large cities had special stores where only foreigners could shop. They accepted only foreign currency. Soviet citizens were forbidden from entering them, much less shopping at them.

ON TO LENINGRAD

Our small group boarded the train called the *Red Arrow* at the Leningrad Rail Station in Moscow for the just over four-hundred-mile train trip to Leningrad. The train pulled out of the station late at night and arrived in Leningrad the following morning. The Soviets' night train state security strategy had worked again—we saw absolutely nothing out the window until arriving at our destination the next morning. Not that there was anything "secret" visible from the train in the first place. But in a police state, one cannot be too cautious about "guarding" state secrets from foreigners and unauthorized personnel.

Odessa's Theatre of Opera and Ballet. Miraculously, during World War II only one corner of this classic old building had been damaged. It was fully restored and remodeled in the 1960s.

Looking down the famous Potemkin staircase toward the port of Odessa. Notice that when viewed from the top of this staircase, only the landings are visible.

View from the bottom of the 155-yard-long Potemkin staircase. Although in this shot (taken in the late afternoon) it is somewhat difficult to see, from the bottom, only the steps are visible. To the left of the staircase is the long escalator that we rode to the top.

Overview of Kiev, showing the Dnepr River and the statue of Saint Vladimir, who baptized the Kievans into the Eastern Orthodox religion in the year 988.

The Hotel "Friendship" where we stayed in Kiev. Again, although some of the signs and billboards in Kiev were in Ukrainian, Russian was the official language and virtually exclusively used there.

A view of the Khreshchatik, Kiev's main thoroughfare as it looked in 1972. Street signs were written, as shown in this photo, in Ukrainian, but Russian was the language we heard on the street.

It was common to name movie theaters (such as this one) after Ukrainian folk heroes, but the movies shown there were all in Russian during the Brezhnev era.

As described earlier in the chapter, we attended a concert conducted in the Kiev Philharmonic Hall by the famous composer Aram Khachaturian, who signed his autograph in English on the program above. It is printed in Ukrainian. An Armenian by birth, Khachaturian spoke Russian with us.

Entrance to the famous Kiev
Pecherska Lavra, where we viewed
the remains of several of the saints
of the Eastern Orthodox Church.
The monastery's renowned bell
tower is to the right.

Red Square in Moscow as it appeared during my last visit there in late October of 1972. Preparations were underway for the celebration of the 55th anniversary of the Russian Revolution. Even more placards, pictures of Lenin, and slogans than usual appeared throughout the country at this time every year during the Soviet era.

Moscow's famous Bolshoi Theatre decorated for the Revolution Day celebrations.

The grave of Soviet leader Nikita Khrushchev as it appeared in 1972. It is rumored that his family had requested a state funeral with burial in the Kremlin Wall, but was denied. Instead, Soviet authorities had this lifelong atheist cynically buried in Moscow in the cemetery of the Russian Orthodox Novodevichy Monastery.

Moscow's famous Gorky Park, where the soda dispensers didn't work very well.

A picture of me on a cold day at Red Square, preparing to visit the Lenin Mausoleum on Halloween day.

LENINGRAD

**"It was much pleasanter at home," thought poor Alice,
"when one wasn't always growing larger and smaller
and being ordered about by mice and rabbits."
—from Lewis Carroll's *Alice in Wonderland***

ARRIVAL IN THE "VENICE OF THE NORTH"

t was early November and our time in Wonderland was beginning to wind down. The weather in Leningrad was turning chilly, and I knew that before the end of our journey we might well face the snows for which this region is famous. Prior to the Russian Revolution, Leningrad had been called Saint Petersburg in honor of its founder—Tsar Peter the Great.[1] Saint Petersburg had been the capital of Tsarist Russia. It was also the seat of Soviet power until 1918 when Lenin moved the capital to Moscow for fear that Petrograd (as it was then known) was too close to the border and thus would make an easier target for foreign invaders.

This is truly a lovely city, which has been called the "Venice of the North," with many narrow canals flowing into the Neva River, which in turn empties into the Bay of Finland on the Baltic Sea. The architecture of the city is stunning, and many of the guides would spend quite a few hours touring it and taking pictures.

We were housed in the old Hotel Astoria, which was first

---

1. During World War I, the city was renamed "Petrograd" to avoid sounding German. After Vladimir Lenin's death in 1924, it was renamed "Leningrad" in his honor. After the fall of the Soviet Union in late 1991, the name again reverted to "Saint Petersburg."

opened in 1912. It was located on Saint Isaac's Square, next to Saint Isaac's Cathedral. My room had a full view of this old church, which, in those years, was not among the "working churches" that conducted services.

The Astoria was built to host tourists who would be visiting Russia in 1913 for the huge celebration of three hundred years of Russian imperial rule by the Romanov Dynasty. This luxurious hotel was used during the celebrations to house guests of the imperial family, and afterwards became a popular spot for the prerevolutionary Russian aristocracy. In 1972, it was still an impressive place, especially compared to some of our other lodgings around the country.

Despite the Astoria's being a fancy place to stay, especially by Soviet standards, I was nevertheless somewhat amazed to discover that one could even order breakfast to be brought to the room. So, the second or third day we were there, I did so. After phoning in my order for kasha and tea, I realized that I had forgotten to ask for bread, so I picked up the receiver to add it. Although by this time in my Soviet journey almost nothing surprised me, still I was taken aback to hear a recording of my voice ordering the meal. Even such mundane things as food orders were monitored and even recorded. Nothing ever slipped past the prying eyes and rabbit ears of the KGB.

We were in our final month in the USSR, and some of the guides had become rather bold. I vividly recall one example of this boldness. Each room in the Astoria had a full-length mirror near the door to check one's appearance before leaving the room. We knew full well that these mirrors were also used by the secret police to monitor our activities and most likely had cameras behind them. One of our more daring guides used to look right into the mirror on his way out of the room and, with a knowing smile on his face, whisper things like "Lenin was a jerk."

This fellow meant these comments as a prank, and when I mentioned to him that, had they wanted, the Soviets could have used his words to cause trouble for him, even to the point of having him declared persona non grata and expelled from the

USSR, his reply was, "So what. Just means I get out of this place a few weeks earlier than planned."

Such a disrespectful act might not have been a polite thing for a foreign guest to do in another country, but I think such behavior was a reaction to the constant pounding we took from the plants at each of our exhibit stops. Nerves were starting to get a bit frayed, as actions such as this revealed.

But, all in all, the accommodations at the Astoria were quite nice. I recall feeling very grateful that Leningrad was the last of our three exhibit cities. Given the creature comforts of the Astoria, it would have been quite a disappointment to have started our Soviet journey here and ended it in Kazan.

SIGHTSEEING IN LENINGRAD

Many of us spent a large portion of such free time as was available to us on touring the city. Leningrad contained so many spectacular edifices—many of them elegant remnants of the prerevolutionary era of the Russian monarchy of which Saint Petersburg was its capital—that it would take a very long chapter just to list and describe them. Therefore, some of these places are included in the photo section at the end of this chapter. Some interesting ones, however, are worth pausing to discuss.

It is important to understand that this city suffered perhaps more than any other in the USSR during World War II. After the German invasion of the country by Adolf Hitler's forces in 1941, the Nazis decided not to attempt to seize Leningrad outright. Rather, Hitler gave the order to surround and lay siege to the city and starve it into submission. It was incessantly bombed and shelled for almost all the years it was surrounded and cut off from the rest of the country. A total blockade was enforced that lasted over nine hundred days, during which approximately one million civilians, including many, many children, perished—the majority from starvation.

Even in 1972, Leningraders, particularly those old enough to remember the war, were especially sensitive to the suffering that had been inflicted upon them and their city. It was against this backdrop that an unfortunate incident occurred that was sad and alarming at the same time. The Soviets organized a day trip for us to visit Peterhof—the glorious palace dedicated to Peter the Great—which is located in the suburbs not far from Leningrad. This beautiful place was badly damaged by the Germans during the war and was restored to its former luster during the postwar era.

Since I spoke German, I sat beside our computer technician—the third and last of those Univac had sent from Germany to help us at the exhibit. He appeared a bit older than the previous two, but it was not until this trip to Peterhof that I realized just how much older. During our bus ride from Leningrad, this fellow suddenly began pointing out to me—in German, of course—some of the places along the route where his artillery unit had been stationed. He said things like "Yes, and it was from here that our battalion laid down barrages of fire and shelled the city." He went on to add more details about the activities of the Germans who had besieged Leningrad for almost three years during the war.

I suddenly noticed that our friend Masha, who was our Soviet tour guide on this trip, had begun listening intently to this guy's story. Because I was not sure how much German she understood, I leaned over to him and whispered in German words to the effect that he needed to stop talking about this matter, at least until we got back to the Astoria. He didn't seem to understand why this was a problem. I thought to myself that one had to have a social tin ear not to get the fact that there was nothing funny, amusing or entertaining about a German soldier talking about his exploits, which included having taken part in the infliction of so much suffering on innocent people during the war. I was very glad when we arrived at Peterhof and I could get this guy away from Masha's staring eyes and radar ears.

The day after our trip to Peterhof and a few days before the exhibit opened, I visited the old Kazan Cathedral dedicated to the Mother of God. After the Russian Revolution in 1917, Soviet authorities closed the cathedral, and in 1932 it reopened as the Museum of the History of Religion and Atheism, which proselytized in favor of atheism and portrayed religion as a relic of the past. By the 1970s, the Soviets had destroyed thousands of churches and converted hundreds of others into alternate purpose facilities, such as had been done with the beautiful Kazan Cathedral.[2]

To have turned this beautiful Russian Orthodox cathedral into a place denigrating religion and praising atheism was an example of how the Soviet regime had waged total war against the church, its priests, and those Russians who wished to practice the religion of their ancestors. The number of martyred Russians from the Soviet era is truly staggering and should give pause to those wishing to deprive anyone from the free exercise of religion, regardless of the reason.

AT THE EXHIBIT

Shortly after our arrival in Leningrad, two events took place on the same day—November 7, 1972: the American presidential election and the celebration of the fifty-fifth anniversary of the October Socialist Revolution.[3]

Since we would not be wearing our political campaign buttons at the exhibit in Leningrad, we began giving them away. I gave mine to an old worker who helped us in the set-up phase before the exhibit opened. He was thrilled to have a souvenir of our visit to his city. The frequent questions about the election would sadly not be asked in Leningrad as they had in Kazan and Donetsk. I say "sadly" because this topic had produced some very interesting conversations on the exhibit floor in the summer and fall.

As we set about unpacking the exhibit items, I was again able to spend time talking with my favorite Soviet interlocutors—the ever-present old men who were there to help unload the smaller

---

2. For an in-depth discussion of the fate of churches, priests, and parishioners during the Soviet era, consult Chapter 10 of the book *The Harvest of Sorrow*, listed in the bibliography.

3. The Russian Revolution took place on October 25, 1917. When the Soviets switched from the Gregorian calendar to the Julian calendar, this was celebrated under the new calendar on November 7.

exhibit items. And from one of them, I heard the best explanation of life under the Soviet regime of that era that I had ever encountered. The elderly gentleman described for me what he called the "system of three." To explain it, he posited a hypothetical situation in which three men had grown up in the same apartment complex and thus had known each other since childhood. In his scenario, these three fellows also worked at the same factory where small parts were manufactured.

One day, according to the old man's story, one of the men—hungover from a night of hard drinking and thus in a foul mood—grabbed a part coming down the conveyor belt where the three were working, swore loudly, and yelled, "Just look at this piece of Soviet junk. It's as worthless as everything else in this godforsaken country of ours."

At this point the "system of three" would kick into gear. The worker's two close friends, who in this hypothetical story were working on either side of him, both know that the other one heard this anti-Soviet outburst from their friend. So, how can either of them know that the other won't report this incident to the secret police? And, were one to do so, the police were sure to call in the one not reporting it and grill him as to why he hadn't informed on the "slanderer."

And here's the kicker. How can either or both of this guy's friends be sure that their buddy hadn't staged this outburst on orders from the secret police to see which of the others would be first to report it to the authorities? As the old man telling the story noted, if you couldn't get three people to trust each other enough to stand up to the Soviet system, how would it be possible to get the thousands it would take to rise up and overthrow it?

This little story exemplified the demonic system of total societal control that Communism had created in the USSR, as well as the stifling effect it had on the average Soviet citizen. I never forgot this example and often used it in lectures I subsequently gave on the Soviet Union of that era.

The daily work at the exhibit in Leningrad proceeded in much the same way it had in our two previous locations. Here, too, a fresh cadre of Soviet undercover plants laid down a daily barrage of questions designed to depict life in the United States in the worst possible light while extolling the virtues of their Socialist utopia. And, as in Donetsk, several of the guides had developed comebacks, often very humorous ones.

For example, one of our guides was being lectured by a plant as to the virtues of East Germany (a Soviet satellite state) and the evils of the "bad Germany" (i.e., America's ally, West Germany). Our guide proceeded to a point at the edge of his exhibit stand and said, "Yes, you're probably right since your friends in the 'good' Germany march like this"—at which point he began goose-stepping across the platform. Reaching the other end, he turned and began walking back the other way in a normal gait, saying, "And this is how our friends in the 'bad' Germany march." The crowd began chuckling, at which point the plant departed and normal discussion of other matters followed.

On more than a few occasions Soviet visitors themselves came to our rescue. One time a plant was giving me a very hard time about the Vietnam War. He asked in a loud voice, "What are you trying to do in Vietnam, save Vietnamese from other Vietnamese?"

There was a very tall young man standing directly behind this plant, who, hearing this non-question, leaned over and said, "Yeah, just like we were saving Czechs from Czechs in 1968."[4]

As often occurred at such moments, the crowd of visitors began chuckling, whereupon the plant started staring at them. Many hurried away, lest they be perceived as agreeing with the young man that the Soviet invasion of Czechoslovakia was unnecessary. But they had tacitly agreed with him as indicated by their laughter.

One event that occurred at our exhibit pavilion on the Vasiliev Island in Leningrad would remain with me for the rest of my life. A discussion between an American guide and a group of Soviet visitors was becoming rather animated. Suddenly, a young

---

4. In 1968, the Soviet military was sent to suppress a popular uprising in Communist Czechoslovakia. They put down this rather peaceful "revolt" with hundreds of Soviet tanks sent from East Germany and Hungary.

Soviet fellow emerged from the crowd and began taking on some of the Soviet plants who had been haranguing the guide with a barrage of standard Marxist-Leninist propaganda talking points. Despite verbal threats from the plants, this young man would not back down, but continued attacking the talking points they were using.

At this point, the young man's wife stepped out of the crowd and began pleading with him to just come home as she tugged at this coat sleeve. But the fellow refused to be deterred from having his say. He pulled his identification papers from his coat and showed them to the American guide. "Look," he said. "I've already done time for expressing my views, and I'm not afraid of being arrested again for it."

The tension in the exhibit hall began to mount. Many visitors in the crowd became quite uneasy. Several of them looked around, seemingly searching for someone or something. I would soon learn why.

From my vantage point at the adjacent Univac stand, I caught sight of the gradual approach of some dour-looking guys in black leather jackets slowly making their way from the back of the pavilion, pushing people out of their way as they moved steadily toward the young man, who was still actively engaged in expressing himself to the American guide. The crowd, sensing what was about to happen, started moving away from the young man. The next thing I noticed was the appearance of a black van at the rear door of the pavilion. One of the men in the van got out and gave what appeared to be a signal to the guys wearing the leather jackets, whereupon they quickly surrounded the young man, grabbed him, roughly whisked him out of the pavilion, and threw him into the black van. Through the glass doors of the pavilion, I saw the van speed away. The crowd of Soviet visitors who had witnessed this event silently dispersed and, with sheepish looks on their faces, walked away.

It was quite a sight. For me, this event was the culmination of all the descriptions of the Soviet Union and Communism that my old Russian teachers had related to me years before. For many of my fellow guides, it was a genuine life-changer as they watched this event unfold and reach its conclusion as the van sped away. It was a clear message to the Soviet visitors not to get too cozy with the Americans working the exhibit and to avoid making inflammatory statements deemed antithetical to the Communist Party and the Soviet Government.

All of us had studied the Soviet Union from afar in college and knew its societal nature. And yet, when young, still somewhat naive Americans see before their eyes someone of their own generation summarily seized by plainclothes secret-police goons and rushed off to an awaiting police van for simply speaking his mind, it is difficult to fully comprehend it. One can read about such things at length, but until they actually witness them in person, the deep meaning of such brutal repression can't be fully understood.

I have often wondered over the years which type of punishment the Soviet authorities chose for this fellow. In those years, there were basically two methods. One way was to simply declare someone expressing anti-Soviet sentiments mentally ill and confine him (against his will, of course) to a psychiatric hospital and administer appropriate "medications" as "treatment" until such a "patient" was deemed "cured" of his disease.[5]

Another method was to expel such a person from his job and record the firing in the person's records. This would blacklist the offender from being hired anywhere else. After such an individual became "unemployed" in this manner, he was deemed a parasite, having violated a Soviet law requiring every citizen to have a job. This would, in turn, inevitably lead to arrest and likely deportation to a Soviet "correctional" labor camp.

Whichever punishment was meted out to the young man for having the audacity to "slander" the USSR in public—and most especially at an American exhibit—I am quite certain it drastically altered his life and that of his poor wife, who sobbed uncontrollably as her husband was being hustled out of the

5. Special psychiatric hospitals for the "treatment" of dissidents were run not by the Soviet Ministry of Health, but by the Ministry of Internal Affairs—a part of the Soviet security apparatus.

exhibit pavilion by KGB goons. This incident was indelibly imprinted on my memory, and as noted, I have thought of it many times over the years. It was the starkest example imaginable of the brutality and oppression wielded by Communism in the old Soviet Union. It was also a visualization of the stark reality of daily life for the average Soviet citizen of that era. It seemed that Stalinism, rather than being dead in the USSR, was still there, lurking just under the surface of everyday life. As mentioned in the preface of this book, I only wish that more members of my generation could have witnessed this example of the brutal reality of Soviet life.

I should note in passing that during the Brezhnev era in the USSR, the use of Stalin's old term "enemy of the people" was dropped. People who disagreed with any aspect of Soviet policy were instead termed "dissidents." The Soviet term for that in Russian was *inakomyslyaschchii*, which literally means "one who thinks differently." To "think differently," you see, was treated as a mental disease since, as Brezhnev himself had once put it, anyone who didn't support Communism and Marxism-Leninism was, by definition, mentally ill and needed to be treated in a psychiatric institution.

On the other end of the spectrum, there was another incident toward the end of our stay in Leningrad. Near our exhibit pavilion was a small dining facility known as a *pel'mennaya*. [6] Several of us often went there for lunch during break time at the exhibit. The shop was very small and always crowded.

As usual in the USSR of that day, there was the typically overcrowded atmosphere of many people pushing, shoving, and yelling. We had become inured to this phenomenon over our nearly six months in the country. But behind the counter of this little shop, one of the employees stood out. She was a young girl, perhaps in her twenties, whose face sported an almost angelic smile. Her good nature and her well-mannered behavior even in this callous atmosphere set her apart from any food server I had encountered in the several areas of the Soviet Union that

---

6. This shop served only Russian *pel'meni*—meat-filled, soft-dough dumplings.

we had visited. I recall thinking how sad it was that we couldn't somehow pluck this lovely flower from this patch of weeds and replant her in the West. She was indeed a rose among the thorns of so many of the Soviet workers I had encountered during my stay in the USSR.

As had become my habit, I was able to leave the Univac display for an hour here and there to work the cars—clearly the most popular and sometimes fun items we displayed. During one such hour, a Soviet visitor was asking me about the price of the three cars we had brought with us from America. During this discussion, I asked the fellow how much a *Zhiguli* cost. He quickly quoted the price—the ruble equivalent of something like $10,000, as I recall. I then asked him how much a *Chaika* cost.[7]

The man paused, and after a minute or so, replied, "That's a government car."

I acknowledged that but again asked him the cost. He repeated his answer, at which point I realized that the matter of the cost of a car available only to government officials never crossed the lad's mind. Since he could never get one, why bother even wondering what it cost?

This man's reaction to my question was another subtle reminder of the duality of the Soviet system. In a country where everyone was supposed to be equal, clearly some were most assuredly more equal than others, to borrow a phrase from author George Orwell. I recall being a bit surprised at the ease with which most average Soviet citizens tacitly accepted this reality.

Near the end of our time in Leningrad, we were invited to a party at the American Consulate. It was here that I let my guard down—something I would pay for later. After we experienced the green tap water in Kazan, I decided to boil water for drinking. In restaurants, I only drank hot tea. This was especially important to do in Leningrad since the city had been built to a large extent on swampland, and the water supply was therefore

---

7. The *Zhiguli* was a Soviet imitation-Fiat, for which an average Soviet worker had to save four or five years of his salary to afford. The *Chaika* was a larger automobile available only to mid-level functionaries of the Soviet Government.

suspect. But here, at an American oasis in a Soviet city, I somehow (naively) imagined that the personnel working at the consulate would have taken this normal precaution. They clearly had not.

I remember putting ice cubes into my cocktail. The water used to make these ice cubes was apparently not boiled, and I came down with internal parasites. They attached themselves to the lining of my stomach and intestines and began "boring in" within a day or two of this event. I thought this was merely a case of indigestion since, after two days of rather severe discomfort, the pain gradually subsided. I thought nothing more about it until after I had returned to the USA a few weeks later. I do recall having lost about fifteen pounds in a matter of a few weeks. The reason turned out to be that the parasites were sharing my food with me. An "exit" medical exam during my outprocessing from the USIA revealed a parasitic infestation, and I was given Atabrine tablets as treatment. This medication, primarily used to treat malaria, was found to be very effective in treating parasitic infestations as well. I soon understood why. This medicine had a horrible taste, and I reasoned that no self-respecting parasite would put up with such treatment. Turns out they didn't—my problem vanished after two weeks of taking this medication. Unfortunately, some quite unneeded extra pounds also returned.

It was from Leningrad that I sent home my last roll of film. For younger readers who likely don't know this process, back in the dinosaur age we used cameras that we loaded with film. Each roll contained a certain number of shots, and when one reached that number, the roll was rewound in the camera, unloaded, and taken to a processing outlet—often a drugstore or other such retail place of business. The film was then "developed" and pictures were produced. My film was sent home via the embassy courier system and was developed and processed into 35mm slides for viewing with a projector.[8]

I would add that the rolls of film were always in my

---

8. These slides were recently digitized, and some have been included in the various chapters as visual examples of the things I saw during my six-month journey.

possession pending shipment home through carrier mail, lest they be tampered with by the Soviets. Such precautions were necessary, thanks to the totally invasive nature of Soviet society in that era.

About a week before the exhibit closed in Leningrad, our group received our exit visas from the Soviet authorities. These documents would allow those holding only an "official" passport to leave the country. They also made it possible for us to make our final travel arrangements with the help of the US Consulate.

I remember noting the easy and hassle-free manner in which we obtained these Soviet exit visas. Upon reflection, I imagine the Soviet authorities were as glad to be rid of us as we were to be departing this place that had become a kind of prison for many of us.

As we loaded up the exhibit items for the last time for shipment back to the West, I enjoyed my final conversations with the Soviet "old-timers" on various subjects. I had truly learned a lot from these people about life in the USSR of that time. Over the coming years, I would often think of them with a sadness that came from knowing that most of them would never live to see the end of the brutal regime that had made their lives so difficult for so long.

Soon it would be time to pack up my personal effects, board a train, and bid a fond farewell to Soviet "Wonderland."

The venerable Hotel Astoria in Leningrad—our accommodations for our last stop in the USSR.

Saint Isaac's Cathedral. My room at the Astoria had a great view of this beautiful church.

Our exhibit pavilion in Leningrad. Note the glass enclosure. This provided us with a "bird's-eye" view of the young man being hauled out of the exhibit and thrown into a police van.

The famous Palace Square. These buildings face the Winter Palace that now houses the world-renowned Hermitage Museum. It was through this archway that the revolutionaries stormed the Winter Palace in 1917 and occupied it in the name of the Bolshevik Party of Vladimir Lenin.

The Winter Palace of the tsars of Russia. It was remodeled after considerable damage was done to the structure by the German Air Force in World War II. This became the Hermitage Museum, housing some of Russia's art treasures assembled from several valuable collections by world-famous artists. During my visit there, I spent three hours touring this magnificent facility. Anyone traveling to Saint Petersburg should definitely stop here.

Part of the huge complex of Peterhof—the summer palace of the Russian tsars—located just outside Leningrad. This was the destination of our bus tour. Unfortunately, I ran out of film after taking this picture. This truly magnificent complex is another place any tourist traveling to Saint Petersburg should definitely plan to visit.

A view of the Neva River from one of the many bridges in Leningrad. This wide river flows into the Gulf of Finland, which is part of the Baltic Sea.

One of the many canals in the city. This view
suggests why it is called the "Venice of the North."

These canals flow into the Neva River and,
ultimately, into the Gulf of Finland and the Baltic
Sea.

The beginning of the parade commemorating the 55th anniversary of the October Socialist Revolution in 1972. This was the Soviet equivalent of our Fourth of July, and people were required to attend.

This picture shows the throng of "volunteers" participating in the parade. Note the float carrying an image of Vladimir Lenin—the founder of the Soviet state. This was all part of the deification of this man who had instituted terror and ruthlessly oppressed all "enemies of the people." Homage to him was mandatory, and he continues to lie in honored repose in the Lenin Mausoleum in Moscow to this day.

More floats and a sea of red flags—all part of the routine of Revolution Day parades throughout the country.

And what would a Soviet parade be without a display of military hardware? This was done to encourage pride among the citizenry in the accomplishments of the glorious Soviet motherland and to demonstrate that the Soviet armed forces stood ready to repulse any imperialist invader.

DEPARTURE FROM WONDERLAND

Well that was the silliest tea party I ever went to!
I am never going back there again!
— from Lewis Carroll's *Alice in Wonderland*

After the exhibit closed in Leningrad, we set about our usual task of dismantling it and helping Soviet workers load it into crates. I have wondered over the years what happened to the display items. Since this was the conclusion of the exhibit, they were probably transported back to Western Europe, with some being returned to the United States. But, knowing how the Soviet system worked, I imagine certain items (especially the smaller ones such as electric knives, can openers, and mixers) were perhaps "damaged in transit" and thus disappeared before they reached the Soviet border. After all, the black market flourished in those years.

Most of the exhibit staff and guides headed home by plane. But five of us felt that to travel directly from Wonderland back to the United States might result in the bends—a problem experienced by scuba and deep sea divers if they rise to the surface too quickly. To avoid this possibility, we decided to travel by train to Helsinki, Finland, and from there to fly to Berlin to "decompress" before returning home.

So on December 19, it was off to Finland Station for our night-train trip out of the USSR. We had done the nocturnal rail trips before, so the ride was rather uneventful until I noticed that the train began gradually slowing down. Something was afoot.

The train came to a full stop on an elevated trestle. From the window, we could see what appeared to be powerful searchlights coming from somewhere below the railroad bridge. This was, in fact, standard operating procedure for Soviet border guards examining trains departing the country. They were training these huge lights on the bottom of the railway cars in search of any daring soul who might have somehow attached himself to the bottom of the train in an effort to flee the Socialist Motherland, aka Wonderland.

A few minutes after the train had come to a full stop, it was boarded by armed Soviet soldiers sporting the same green epaulets I had seen upon arrival at the airport in Moscow. These border guard troops quickly entered our compartment, checked our passports and visas, and proceeded to rifle through our luggage and personal belongings. They were on the lookout for any contraband such as Russian religious icons or other such "items of national treasure."[1] If such were found on the person of someone traveling on an official US passport (such as we had), I'm sure the offender would have been hauled off the train and escorted to a waiting military police van, similar to what had happened to the young man at the exhibit in Leningrad.

While this process probably only lasted about five minutes, it seemed to take forever, perhaps because the stone-faced border guards appeared more diligent in their search than the customs officials had been at the Moscow airport when we arrived. After being "behind the wire," as it were, in the hermetically sealed USSR for six months, I felt my palms getting sweaty during the search of our luggage, even though I knew I didn't have any "prohibited items" in my possession. I thought, *What if someone planted contraband in my bag to delay my departure from this place?* I was developing a Soviet-like paranoia after only six months.

To my great relief, such paranoid thoughts did not bear fruit, and the soldiers left our compartment and headed farther down the corridor to check the other passengers. I did not see them exit

---

1. We had been warned about trying to buy such items on the black market during our training in Washington. This was part of a rigged game the Soviets played whereby their agents would try to sell such "prohibited" items to tourists, then confiscate them at the border and resell them again and again to unsuspecting foreigners.

the train, but after what seemed like another eternity, the train suddenly jolted and began to gradually pick up speed. Could it be that we would soon be free of the pervasive eyes of Big Brother?

As the train resumed full speed, we sat nervously at the window and within a few minutes caught sight of a billboard alongside the tracks. It was an advertisement—in Finnish—with a picture of a Volkswagen. At that moment, we knew that we had crossed the border and were in Finland. Free at last, free at last! I can barely describe the joyful feeling that enveloped me.

What ensued was a scene I had witnessed only once before, in Donetsk when the Canadian national hockey team had defeated the Soviet team, setting off a raucous celebration on TV. My buddies started pulling out champagne bottles that we had purchased on the train, and the celebration was on.

People who have never spent time in prison or similarly protracted confinement probably can't relate to our feelings at that moment. For six long months we had been confined to staying within the boundaries of what was a totally closed society. Our only lifeline to the outside world was through letters from home and information received from the US embassy in Moscow.

Upon arriving in Helsinki the next morning, we grabbed our carry-on bags and headed out into the city.[2] The first thing that struck me was how alive the city was. There seemed to be thousands of cars on the street, and we gawked at the colorful attire of the people. I noticed how they seemed animated and like they were enjoying themselves, unlike the drab, gloomy, and sullen mood of so many of the Soviet people we had encountered in the USSR. I recall also being pleased at the absence of political slogans and the colorless, heavy, and stoic atmosphere to which we had become accustomed in Soviet Wonderland.

Walking down the street, we came to a restaurant and peered inside through a large bay window. People were eating breakfast, and I caught sight of bacon, ham, eggs, and what appeared to

---

2. I had sent most of my things home through the embassy route and was "traveling light," with only those items of clothing and personal hygiene I needed for the three days of my travel home to the USA.

be real milk. As I rushed into the restaurant, my nostrils were filled with wonderful culinary smells that I hadn't experienced since my last trip to the American embassy commissary some six weeks before.

We quickly occupied a table, and in what seemed like record time compared to the virtual eternity of the dining process in the USSR, there suddenly appeared before us a veritable feast consisting of all the aforementioned goodies. I wolfed down my food like a starving vagabond who hadn't eaten in weeks. While I'm sure I stuffed myself to excess, the main thing I remember about that meal is how much I had missed such gastronomic delights for what seemed to have been forever.

Looking back on this event, I imagine the Finns in the restaurant were asking themselves what manner of strange creatures had invaded their city. I'm sure they were taken aback at our disheveled appearance and lack of civilized table manners. The Martians had landed.

ON TO BERLIN

That afternoon, we boarded a Lufthansa jet for the brief flight to Berlin, where we would "decompress" for a couple of days before flying back to the United States. Little did we know that another genuine adventure awaited us. We checked into the Hilton Berlin hotel and turned in early for some badly needed rest. The next morning, our small group headed out for some sightseeing and our "adventure" began.

From our hotel, we started walking east in the direction of the Berlin Wall. A few minutes into our walk, a West German policeman drove by in a Volkswagen, slowed down, and gave us a long look. He then sped away.

Strange, I thought. We continued on our way.

As we were about to cross the street and approach the Wall where the Soviet War Memorial was located in East Berlin, several West German police vehicles suddenly came screeching out of the woodwork with lights and sirens.

"I wonder what they're doing here," I said to my friends.

Well, it turned out that *we* were what they were doing there. Before we knew it, all five of us were frisked and loaded into the back of a windowless police van, which then sped off. Two armed West German policemen sat near the door of the van with their loaded weapons pointed in our direction. When we started asking each other what the heck was happening, one of the officers loudly said in German, "*Schweigen!*"—which means "Shut up!"

We complied and rode quietly to our destination, which turned out to be a local precinct station of the West German Criminal Police. We were rousted out of the van, put up against it, and again frisked. I tried to show the officers my American passport, but they were not interested in talking with us. Instead, they seized our passports and hustled us inside the station, where we were placed in separate cells.

As I was sitting in that West German holding cell, I began thinking how ironic this was. We had just come through six months of being behind the barbed wire—physically and psychologically. Now, on our second day of "decompression" from that experience, here we were, sitting behind bars in a free country.

About ten minutes later, a peephole in the large wooden cell door opened and a young lady looked me up and down.

Oh, my God, I thought. *This doesn't look good!*

Several more minutes passed without further action. With my patience growing thin, I began loudly demanding that the US consul be called. Shortly thereafter, the precinct commander opened the doors and let each of us out. His formerly gruff attitude had completely changed. He meekly explained to me in German that there had been an unfortunate mistake and told us how profoundly sorry he was about it. He then outlined what had happened.

As it turned out, a few minutes after we had left the Hilton Berlin on our walk, four armed men entered a jewelry store adjacent to the hotel and robbed it at gunpoint. One of the men, according to the police, was dressed in a green military-style field jacket. And, indeed, one of our guys was dressed in such a coat that morning. Thus, this was an unfortunate case of mistaken identity.

After all this excitement and since we hadn't had breakfast, the five of us were famished. We asked the police to please take us to a restaurant so we could have brunch. They complied. Reasoning that they would be most accommodating to us after their foul-up, I also requested that they wait until we finished our meal and then drive us back to where we had been picked up so we could resume our sightseeing. They were most happy to comply with this small request, too.

The next morning an article appeared in the Berlin section of the *Tagesspiegel*—a West German newspaper. The headline read "Four Masked Men Robbed a Jeweler in the Hilton Complex." The article indicated that "Five young men were picked up by the police from the Tiergarten area [of Berlin] for questioning in this case. They were later released since they clearly had no connection to the crime."

Over the years I kept a copy of this article in case our "adventure" were ever to come up after we left Berlin. Happily, it never did. But to say that the five of us were scared out of our wits that morning is an understatement of colossal proportions.

The rest of our time in Berlin was taken up with the usual tourist-type things: sightseeing, enjoying German cuisine, and taking pictures, including a few showing the infamous wall that divided the city and imprisoned East Berliners from 1961 until it was torn down in 1989.

At the Wall, I recall looking eastward into East Berlin and thinking how similar it was to the Soviet Union I had recently left. How sad that so many innocent people were trapped behind these barriers in so many Communist countries and forced to live under a system from which they could not escape. This image has remained fresh in my mind's eye to this day.

Our group wanted to get home for Christmas, so the next day we boarded a flight for Frankfurt, West Germany, and from there flew back to America. My half-year-long odyssey had come to an end, and I was more than ready to get home and set about finding a permanent job, hopefully one involving Russian in some fashion.

Six months after my return, my still-youthful life came full circle. I was hired to teach Russian at the very place where my Russian language career had begun: the Defense Language Institute in beautiful Monterey, California. My tour of duty in the Soviet Union had greatly benefited my language proficiency and completed the foundation on which I was able to build a career doing something I had hoped to do since early in my youth—using and teaching foreign languages.

All in all, I'd say the time I spent in "Wonderland" was well worth the inconveniences and hardships it entailed. It turned out to be an invaluable experience I would never forget. I can honestly say, decades later, that, while I wouldn't do it again, I also would not trade it for the world.

A shot of the Berlin Wall showing a "death zone" and a guard tower. Note the contrast between Communism and the West. Such barriers as these kept people locked up in their Socialist paradises.

Guard towers ran the entire length of the Berlin Wall. The guards had orders to shoot anyone approaching the impenetrable fortifications of these "forbidden zones." Many tried and lost their lives in the process.

The historic Brandenburg Gate as viewed from just west of the Wall. Germans used to joke that the chariot atop the gate was headed in the wrong direction, and that if the driver had any sense, he'd turn around and head west. The flag atop the gate was that of East Germany, and the flag to the right was the Soviet flag.

The Soviet Military War Memorial in East Berlin as viewed from an area just west of the Wall. This memorial was manned 24/7/365 by Soviet soldiers and was a constant reminder to the East Berliners of who had conquered Berlin in 1945 and who ultimately was still in charge of their country.

ON THE LIGHTER SIDE

Imagination is the only weapon in the war against reality.
—Jules de Gaultier

L ife in the old Soviet Union was, as a rule, a miserable existence for those whose only offense was the misfortune of having been born there. As one old-timer explained to me, when you live in a society where the individual is completely subordinated to the collective, and from which there is literally no escape, you have to find ways to survive.

Sadly, one way was through alcohol. During my four years of active duty in the US Army, I was hardly an advocate of abstinence from alcohol. But what I observed over six months in nine Soviet cities convinced me that the people trapped there probably spilled more alcohol by accident than we young soldiers had ever intentionally consumed.

Another method of escape from Socialist reality for a very large number of Soviet citizens was humor. I regret not having had a handheld tape recorder with me on my trip. I probably heard at least two hundred jokes during my six-month stay in the USSR. The gist of a few of them I was able to scribble down on a pad of paper, and others just stuck in my mind due to how funny (and totally fitting) they were.

In this chapter, I retell some of the best of these anecdotes, including some cultural references to help explain why they were so funny (and so appropriate to Soviet society of that era).

LEONID BREZHNEV—THE BUTT OF MANY JOKES

In 1964, Leonid Ilyich Brezhnev, an old-time party hack, replaced Nikita Khrushchev as General Secretary of the Politburo of the Central Committee of the Communist Party of the Soviet Union—the most powerful post in the USSR. While he nominally shared power with Alexei Kosygin, Brezhnev was clearly the "top man" and the "boss of the bosses" of the Kremlin. He would hold that position until his death in 1982. Brezhnev drank heavily, spoke Russian with a Ukrainian-style accent, and, whether from the effects of oceans of vodka or health problems, tended to slur his words.

I heard numerous jokes (sometimes in whispered tones) about Brezhnev, who was still in power during my trip in 1972. I can't recall how many Brezhnev jokes I heard that year, but here are a couple of the best ones I remember:

One fantastic Brezhnev joke involved his then ninety-plus-year-old mother. As the joke went, Brezhnev invited his mother to the Kremlin to show her all that he had achieved in his life. He proudly showed her his huge Kremlin office with the thick carpets on the floor, the luscious paneling on the walls, the beautiful chandeliers hanging from the high ceilings, and the many impressive-looking telephones on his enormous desk. She looked around, but said nothing.

Strange, thought Brezhnev. Well, he'd show her. Next, he took her to his *dacha* (country house) outside Moscow and showed her his luxurious digs there, including a virtual stable of Mercedes and other expensive foreign cars that he had collected over the years. This, too, failed to produce a reaction from his mother.

Becoming exasperated at his mother's apathy, Brezhnev then took her by private jet to his summer residence in the Crimea and showed her around his huge mansion. When his mother again failed to show any reaction, Brezhnev, now quite irate, thundered, "Mama! What's wrong with you? I showed you my impressive office in the Kremlin, my wonderful *dacha* near Moscow, and this palatial residence of mine here in the Crimea, but you just look around silently. Say something!"

To which his elderly mother in her peasant dialect replied,

"This is all wonderful, son, but watch out. The Bolsheviks may come back and take it all away."

***

Another typical Brezhnev joke had the Soviet leader storming into the office of his personal secretary and angrily demanding that the authorities investigate a rumor that had surfaced to the effect that a special commemorative Leonid Brezhnev postal stamp was not sticking to the envelopes.

The Soviet bureaucrat immediately began a thorough investigation and returned two weeks later to Brezhnev and nervously reported: "Comrade Brezhnev. It is true that your stamp is not sticking to the envelopes, and the only reason we could find was that people are apparently spitting on the wrong side of the stamp."

After Nikita Khrushchev's famous 1956 speech denouncing the excessive brutality of Soviet dictator Josef Stalin, it became easier to tell Stalin jokes. I recall hearing two:

The first one had Stalin pacing back and forth in his Kremlin office when his personal secretary entered the room. Stalin said, "I can't find my pipe. Someone must have broken in here and stolen it. Look into it."

Stalin's secretary clicked his heels and set about conducting an exhaustive investigation as to the missing pipe. A week later, he attempted to report his findings to Stalin, who said, "Never mind about the pipe. I found it."

His secretary then said, "That's interesting, Comrade Stalin, because in just one week's time, forty-five suspects confessed to having stolen it."

***

The other told of a situation involving a trip Stalin was making through the countryside. His entourage reached a small town, and the head of the local Communist Party there told Stalin that he had arranged a brief visit to a local facility. That turned out to be a mental institution, and when Stalin was escorted into a large hall, the residents of the facility broke into a loud ovation, yelling over and over: "Hurray for Comrade Stalin."

Stalin noticed that everyone had participated in this exercise except one fellow standing off to the side of the large group. On his way out of the building, Stalin passed by this man and whispered to him, "All the others were cheering me, but you were silent. Why?"

The man nervously answered, "Pardon me, Comrade Stalin, but I'm not crazy—I just work here."

This joke may be considered inappropriate in America, but it was very typical of the kind of dark humor that characterized Soviet life of the 1970s.

Even the "great" Vladimir Lenin, the founder of the Soviet state, couldn't (posthumously) escape jokes. One of the better known of these refers to the monument in front of Saint Basil's Cathedral in Moscow.[1] This monument depicts Kuzma Minin pointing something out to Prince Dmitri Pozharsky. Minin's finger is pointing in the direction of the Lenin Mausoleum. Legend has it that one day someone wrote in chalk on the base of this monument "That's where the dog is buried," in clear reference to Lenin lying in the mausoleum.

EVERYDAY LIFE IN THE SOVIET UNION

By far, the jokes I heard most often concerned life in general in the Soviet Union. I will attempt to relate a few of them here, adding cultural context for clarity.

Soviet political theory taught that workers and peasants had revolted against capitalism and created a Socialist state that would, in time, evolve into Communism. One humorous saying was that communist theoreticians should have first tried the glorious experiment of Socialism on laboratory animals before inflicting it on humans.

As mentioned in an earlier chapter, another such joke on this subject went like this: "It turns out that Marxist theorists

---

1. See the picture section at the end of the chapter entitled "Arrival in Moscow."

left out an intermediate step along the way from Socialism to Communism—alcoholism!"

Alcoholism was indeed rampant in the old Soviet Union, and there is no way I can remember all the jokes about it that were told to me. Some of these require a bit of context to get the point of the joke and fully appreciate it.

My favorite joke about Soviet drinking dealt with a scenario in which a western researcher had been granted permission to visit a Soviet factory to study the effects of alcohol on labor productivity in the USSR. He sits down with a Soviet laborer, explains the study, and then pulls out a large bottle of vodka, pours the worker a full glass, and asks him whether he could drink the whole glass and still work. The Soviet worker, astounded by his good fortune, gulps down the entire glass of straight vodka and says, "Yep. I can still work."

After writing a few things in his notebook, the researcher pours a second full glass of vodka and asks, "How about after a second glass?"

The worker gleefully chugs the second glass and slowly, deliberately says that, yes, he can still work.

"Okay," says the researcher, "How about after a *third* full glass of vodka?"

Smiling, the worker downs the third glass and sets it on the table.

"Can you still work?" he's asked.

"Nope," answers the worker. "But I can supervise."

***

Some jokes were quite short—almost one-liners. Here are a couple of examples:

"We pretend to work, and they pretend to pay us."

***

"Soviet social scientists have established that Adam and Eve must have been Soviet Russians since they were half-naked, had no roof over their heads, shared an apple a day for food, and thought they were in paradise."

POLITICAL JOKES

Numerous Soviet-era jokes turned on political themes. One involved a hypothetical conversation between an American and a Soviet citizen:

American: "I live in a country where, if I want to, I can walk right up to the White House and scream that the President of the United States is a complete jerk."

Soviet citizen: "So what? I live in a country where I can walk right out onto Red Square and scream that the President of the United States is a complete jerk."

An alternate version had the Soviet citizen saying: "So what? I can walk right out onto Red Square and call the General Secretary of the Communist Party a complete jerk—*one* time."

***

One funny little story shows how sarcastically many Soviet citizens regarded the nature of the "New Soviet Man"—the myth that Socialism had created a totally new and exalted species of humans. It went like this:

One day a peasant was tilling the soil on a collective farm when his plow hit something hard. The guy stops his horse, looks down, and sees a strange object upon which was written "Aladdin's magic lamp—rub for a wish." The little fellow rubs the lamp and, sure enough, out pops a genie who says, "Your wish is my command. What would you like?"

The peasant says, "Well, my neighbor has a cow."

The genie asks, "Would you like a cow, too?"

To which the guy says, "No. I want you to kill my neighbor's cow."

***

Russians even told satirical jokes of the gallows-humor variety.

For example, here are a couple of jokes I heard concerning Soviet forced labor camps:

A new prisoner arrives at a work camp and asks an old-timer, "Hey, Grandpa, can one pray to God here?"

The old guy answers, "Yeah, but it's best if God is the only one to hear you do it."

***

And then there was this:

An old-timer in one of the GULAG camps asks a new arrival, "How many years did you get?" (referring to the guy's prison sentence).

The newcomer says, "Twenty-five years."

The old-timer then asks, "What did you do?"

The new prisoner says, "Well, that's just it—I didn't do anything!"

The oldster smiles wryly and says, "Liar! You only get ten years for that!"

***

Another such joke centered around a fellow who had just been sentenced to a long term of exile at a labor camp. After his sentencing, the man asked the judge, "Your Honor, which regime runs that camp?"

The judge answered, "Well, it's a Soviet camp, of course."

The prisoner then asked, "Then could you send me into exile a bit farther away?"

***

The Soviets always ballyhooed their "free health care" system. This was also the butt of more than a few jokes. My favorite told of a patient being wheeled into the emergency room of the main hospital in Moscow. Doctors gathered around him, and one said, "Shall we treat this guy or let him live?"

***

As has been pointed out previously, the city of Leningrad was founded in the early eighteenth century by Russian Tsar Peter the Great and was named in his honor (Saint Petersburg). During World War I, its name was changed to Petrograd to give it a more Russian flavor versus the German-sounding Saint Petersburg. After the Russian Revolution of 1917, it was renamed in honor of the founder of the Soviet state, Vladimir Lenin, and became Leningrad.

There was a joke about this that had an old man sitting in a restaurant in Leningrad, drinking quite a bit and sobbing. The waiter asked him what was wrong.

The old guy said, "Well, I was born in Saint Petersburg," whereupon he took another big slug of vodka and resumed his sobbing.

The waiter asked, "So what?"

The fellow then said, "Then I lived in Petrograd," and gulped down another glass of vodka and again began weeping inconsolably.

The exasperated waiter then shouted, "So, what do you want?"

Through his tears, the old man said, "I just want to go back to Saint Petersburg."

***

Some political jokes also focused on the Soviet media. Examples:

The two major newspapers in the USSR were *Pravda* (the Russian word for "truth") and *Izvestiya* (Russian for "news"). The humorous saying was "There's no 'news' in the 'Truth' and no 'truth' in the 'News'."[2]

***

Then there was the story about two sprinters. The context of this joke concerns how TASS—the official Soviet wire

---

2. In Russian, this play on words is: *"V Pravde nyet izvestii; v Izvestiyakh nyet pravdy."*

service—would report the results of sporting events. The joke focuses on the reporting of the results of a two-man race in the hundred-meter dash, which TASS reports as if this race took place at a huge international track meet with many contestants. The results of this race would be reported differently, depending on which sprinter won.

If the Soviet sprinter won the race, TASS would report it as follows: "At a huge international sporting event, in the hundred-meter dash, the Soviet sprinter finished first, with the American sprinter finishing last."

If the American sprinter won the race, TASS would report: "At a huge international sporting event, in the hundred-meter dash, the Soviet sprinter finished second, with the American sprinter finishing next to last."

Thus, it was, thanks to Soviet news reporting, a "win-win" for the Soviets and a "lose-lose" for the Americans. In addition to being clever, this joke was closer to reality than most people in the West could imagine.

Soviet foreign policy did not escape the wit of the jokesters, either. One such joke concerned the mode of transportation employed by Soviet citizens:

Question: How do most Soviet citizens travel around their cities?

Answer: By bus, streetcar, or trolley.

Question: How do Soviet citizens travel around the USSR?

Answer: By plane or by train.

Question: How do Soviets travel abroad?

Answer: In tanks.[3]

And so it went, on and on, joke after joke. The ones included here are but a sample of the hundreds of jokes I heard from Soviet citizens during my six-month trek through Socialist Wonderland. I must admit that, given the harsh reality of their daily lives, it was a tribute to them that they were able to maintain any semblance of a sense of humor.

Hopefully this chapter has provided a bit of comic relief about

---

3. A clear allusion to the Soviets' deployment of its military to suppress uprisings such as in Hungary in 1956 and in Czechoslovakia in 1968.

a country that, all things considered, wasn't exactly what one would call "funny." Jokes in the old USSR showed how a captive people could exercise humor to comment on life in their highly restricted environment. One guy told me, "Without jokes, we'd probably cry a lot more, and many of us would go nuts."

***

**"My dear, here we must run as fast as we can,
just to stay in place.
And if you wish to go anywhere
you must run twice as fast as that."
—from Lewis Carroll's *Alice in Wonderland***

EPILOGUE

*If you board the wrong train, it is no use running
along the corridor in the other direction.*
— German theologian and dissident from the Nazi era
Dietrich Bonhoeffer

Over the years I have thought many times of my adventures in the USSR. My six-month odyssey in what Soviet emigres often referred to as "Wonderland" was indeed a pivotal point in my life. At age twenty-five, I thought I'd seen pretty much everything the world had to offer after four years in the army, a little over two of which were spent in Germany. But it is truly eye-opening for people born into and raised under a system characterized by individual freedom and personal liberty to witness firsthand what life is like in a closed, totalitarian society.

My only personal exposure to the Soviet system prior to this journey had come through the headsets I wore at an Army Security Agency listening post in West Germany while monitoring the activities of Soviet military units stationed across the border in East Germany. But 1972 provided me with an "up close and personal" view of that system. For me, the most illustrative example of the cavernous difference between a free society and one ruled by the iron fist of totalitarianism was and remains in my memory to this day the seizing of the young man at the exhibit in Leningrad. The USSR had been hermetically sealed since the 1920s, walled off and isolated from the rest of the world by barbed wire and minefields. The KGB was in full control of every aspect of Soviet life, as illustrated by the old fellow in Leningrad's story about the "system of three."

At the time of writing this book, forty-five years have elapsed since my trip to the Soviet Union. Little did we know at the close of 1972 that within a mere nineteen years after our departure, the monolithic communist state would collapse, liberating the people of the fifteen so-called republics comprising the USSR, as well as those living in Soviet client states in Eastern Europe. As columnist Mark Steyn succinctly put it: "The assumption of permanence is the illusion of every age."

None of us who had served in Europe in the US military of the 1960s or spent time in the Soviet Union during the 1970s could have foreseen in our wildest dreams the demise of that totalitarian behemoth. William F. Buckley's prophetic words at the dinner in Donetsk were the only truly accurate predictions I had ever heard on the subject.[1]

In an interview with the producers of a 1998 CNN documentary entitled "The Cold War," Czech dissident writer and first president of the post-Communist Czech Republic, Václav Havel, said of Communism: "Something that goes against life may last a long time, but sooner or later it will collapse." And the Soviet empire in Russia and Eastern Europe did indeed disintegrate in the final decade of the twentieth century.

I recall President Ronald Reagan calling the Soviet Union an "evil empire" in the early 1980s. This was ironic in the sense that since the earliest days of the lead-up to the Russian Revolution in the early twentieth century, through the entire history of the USSR, and virtually until its ultimate dissolution in 1991, Marxist-Leninist doctrine taught that it was the capitalist West that had oppressed and exploited working people. So Reagan was completely correct in pointing out the oppressive nature of the Soviet Union, even though he was roundly criticized for doing so.

Years after my trip to Wonderland, I discovered the following quote concerning the society I had personally visited in 1972:

In my study of communist societies, I came to the conclusion that the purpose of communist propaganda was not to persuade

---

1. Again, Mr. Buckley, when asked about the fate of the Soviet Union, answered simply: "It's imperiled."

or convince, nor to inform, but to humiliate; and therefore, the less it corresponded to reality the better. When people are forced to remain silent when they are being told the most obvious lies, or even worse when they are forced to repeat the lies, they lose their sense of probity.... One's standing to resist anything is thus eroded, and even destroyed.[2]

This quote reminds me of the reaction of the old man in Riga after reading aloud the slogans that appeared in huge letters atop nearby buildings. And there was the stark contrast between the article in *Pravda* praising the "record harvest" of 1972 and the almost empty bread section in the miners' dining facility in Donetsk, above which hung a sign that read "Take only the bread you need for your meal; Bread is a treasure—conserve it." During virtually the entire reign of the Communist Party in the USSR, generations of people, realizing that things were unlikely to change in their lifetimes, were forced to accept the blatant hypocrisy of Soviet propaganda and go about their dreary daily lives despite it.

The only effective antidote to such mind-numbing propaganda is truth. As the old saying goes, "Sunlight is the best disinfectant." And, in a small way, we who served in the old USIA cultural exchange exhibit program did provide a bit of sunshine by telling ordinary Soviet citizens a different side of America's story from that with which they were constantly bombarded in the Soviet media, in Soviet schools, and by the Soviet Government.

Over the years since my return to the United States, I've had the opportunity to work with many former Soviet citizens. Space does not permit me to share all the things they related to me about life in that place—only some of which I had seen with my own eyes in 1972. Two instances remain in my memory as examples of the lasting scars Soviet Communism left on people.

The first occurred during a conversation with a woman who had grown up in Leningrad. She was discussing life in the USSR and suddenly said, "You know, it's strange. Many of us [former

2. British author and social commentator Anthony Daniels, who writes under the pseudonym Theodore Dalrymple.

Soviet citizens] are still afraid." I asked her what she feared. Her answer was indicative of the lasting effect of living under totalitarianism. She said, "I don't know. But we are still afraid."

The other is a personal story that I found to be totally revealing of the brutal reality that was the Soviet Union. An elderly former Soviet citizen told me how he had come to lose his left arm. He had spent time in the infamous GULAG, and frostbite had claimed his arm. He said that his most vivid recollection of those years was when the guards came into the barracks at dawn one cold, snowy winter morning and rousted the (political) inmates, herding them outside for their morning formation. They were given long poles, then marched deep into a dense forest, and ordered to knock ice accumulations off the trees.

During a rest break a few hours into their assignment, this man had occasion to strike up a conversation with a young KGB guard. He told the guard that he was not surprised that the prisoners were forced to work, but asked if it wouldn't perhaps be better if they were given something productive to do, rather than the inexplicably inane chore of knocking ice off trees in a remote and deserted forest. The guard sneered and replied, "You still don't understand? We don't need you to work. We need you to suffer."

And suffer the Soviet people did—through revolution, Lenin's terror, civil war, secret-police repression, "corrective" labor camps, Stalin's Great Terror fed by his paranoid delusions that created a hell on earth, political persecution, deprivation, famine, constant police harassment and persecution, imprisonment of the innocent, and substandard economic conditions with frequent shortages of basic consumer goods routinely available in the West. As retired Soviet and Russian General Dmitri Volkogonov wrote, the Soviet Union was founded on "Bolshevik ways, ways that were based on class cruelty, confrontation, and the cultivation of the lie."[3]

---

3. As the Director of the Soviet Institute of Military History, Volkogonov had full access to a wide array of Soviet archives and based his historical treatise, *Autopsy for an Empire*, on them (see bibliography).

All this and more was endured by people who, like the vast majority of their ancestors, had never experienced individual liberty. For generations of Soviet citizens, "self-determination" was just another in a long line of meaningless propaganda slogans used against the West during the Cold War in the Soviets' effort at spreading Communism throughout the world. The term had absolutely no relationship to the manner in which the USSR itself was governed.

In 1991, the longsuffering Russian people were finally able to throw off the chains of their many decades of Communist oppression. Unfortunately, in the 1990s, the transition from a completely closed, authoritarian society to an open, democratic country was less than smooth. Boris Yeltsin—himself an old Communist apparatchik—heralded the fall of the Soviet Union as a joyous time of freedom for the Russian people. However, Yeltsin must have known that Soviet Russians had never had a say in how their country was governed. Only twice in recorded history had Russians enjoyed any form of democracy: in the Novgorod Republic of ancient times and during a very brief period of semi-democracy after the abdication of the last Russian Tsar—Nicholas II—in 1917. How, then, could they be expected to instantly participate in a free and open democracy?

Suddenly, after centuries of autocratic rule and seventy-four years of totalitarian dictatorship and oppression, the Russian people were asked to chart the course of their own lives. Sadly, as the decade of the 1990s would prove, they were simply not prepared psychologically and societally to chart that course through the admittedly messy business of democratic self-rule. A grave mistake was made in the transformation away from totalitarianism to democracy. Unlike postwar Germany in 1945, the demise of the Soviet Union was not accompanied by a period of thoughtful self-analysis and societal purification, as it were. Since Russia remained a nuclear superpower, no external force was going to require them to administer justice to the officials who had overseen the infliction of so much repression and violence against their "enemies," as had been done with former Nazi officials in postwar Germany.

This meant that numerous secret police and Communist Party officials, instead of being held accountable for their roles in propagating the long history of Soviet crimes against humanity, were permitted in postcommunist Russia to retire into seclusion and peacefully live out their lives. This was a colossal injustice that Russia and the world have never come to grips with.

Many Russians nowadays mockingly refer to the fledgling democracy of the 1990s as "dermocracy," which would roughly translate to "crapocracy."[4] It was natural for Russians, given their long subjection to autocracy, to revert to it. This partially explains the rise and current popularity of Russian President Vladimir Putin.

These and other related factors combine to explain how it came to be that Russia has to date been unsuccessful in moving from a totalitarian system to a free, truly democratic one. As Russian historian Dmitri Volkogonov put it, "All of Russia's misfortunes stem from the fact that she was never able to come to terms with liberty."[5]

At the time of the writing of this book, numerous stories about Russia have made their way into the news in America. What has been lost in the hectic twenty-four-hour news cycle is the virtual impossibility of accurately understanding Russia and her current role in the world without an in-depth study of the society that produced today's Russian Federation. Absent this historical link, it is unlikely that those in the West will ever comprehend the motives and intentions of the current Russian leadership.

History indeed has many lessons to teach us, but, as Aldous Huxley was quoted as having said: "That men do not learn much from the lessons of history is the most important of all the lessons of history." As stated in the preface of this book, among my intended audience are the growing numbers of Americans who are too young to remember the Soviet Union. There is much

---

4. This concocted word is built upon the Russian word *dermo*, which means "excrement" or, colloquially, "crap."
5. *Autopsy for an Empire*, by Dmitri Volkogonov (1998), page 432.

that Americans can and should learn from the history of the USSR.

What I saw and experienced in that society, as well as what we now see in places such as Communist North Korea and Socialist Venezuela, combine to remind me of the wisdom of the oft-cited notion that a government big enough to give you everything you want is big enough to take away everything you have. It seems this refers not only to materials things, but also to a person's freedom, rights, and privileges. Such blessings are either guaranteed by the rule of law, or they will be subject to the whims of a powerful government.

Although I can barely remember the days of my youth as a teen, I do understand the lure of promises to "transform" America into a society where, it is argued, we can link arms and join the "struggle" for concepts such as social justice, income equality, and other utopian outcomes. However, a study of history reveals how Socialists and Communists have played on these themes for centuries. It also clearly shows that the societies they created have never ended well.

Now, in the twilight of my life, as I begin my eighth and likely final decade here on earth, I feel an obligation to add my personal experiences from 1972 to the historical record. Although some may perceive it as such, this book is not primarily intended to be a political or ideological treatise. Rather, it is my hope that by reflecting on the examples of Soviet life provided in this book, the reader—and most especially the young reader—will develop a sense of the relevance of history to decision-making about the future.

Hopefully, free people in the West will avail themselves of the wisdom of an old Russian proverb: "Measure the cloth seven times before making the first cut." Would that the Russian people had followed this advice themselves in 1917.

In his comprehensive treatise on Soviet history, General Volkogonov wrote the following:

For many years I was an orthodox Marxist, and it was only late in my life, after a long and tortuous inner struggle, that I was able to free myself of the chimera of Bolshevik ideology.

I felt enormous relief, and at the same time a sense of deep regret that I had wasted so many years in Utopian captivity.... Disillusionment first came to me as an idea.... Finally, [it came] as the determination to confront the truth and understand it."[6]

It is my fervent hope that future generations of Americans won't have to look back upon their lives as this Russian general's conscience forced him to do in his later years. One way to avoid having to do that is to carefully consider the path we are currently traveling in light of documented tragedies such as the oppression that Soviet Communists foisted upon so many innocent people for over seventy years in the twentieth century.

Lenin, Lenin, everywhere. Images of this Soviet figure were on display throughout the entire Soviet Union for over seventy years. He was seen in every Soviet classroom, on buildings, in offices, and on monuments as part of the deification of this man and the supposed infallibility of the system he created. These images were also constant reminders of the power and presence of Big Brother.

---

6. *Autopsy for an Empire* by Dmitri Volkogonov, page xxvi.

While portrayed as a friendly father figure, Lenin, who banned all noncommunist parties, also established a dictatorship, instituting terror as a mechanism to control the people. He was revered by Soviet myth as a great man and a successful leader. Lenin started his country down a path that led to the slaughter of countless millions of innocent people and yet was glorified by the Soviet state. Sadly, to this day his body still lies in honored repose in the Lenin Mausoleum on Moscow's Red Square.

The ever-present, mythical figure of Lenin—the man whose word was law in the USSR—seemed even after his death to be personally supervising every aspect of Soviet life. Thus the Soviet slogan "Lenin lived, Lenin lives, Lenin will live." It was a classic case of the kind of society George Orwell famously described in his book 1984.

As early as 1913, Vladimir Lenin had said that the very thought of God or religion was "unspeakable vileness." After the revolution, he set about destroying churches, killing priests, and waging an all-out war against the Russian Orthodox Church. Tens of thousands of churches were either destroyed or converted to other uses such as skating rinks and museums promoting the wisdom of atheism. Countless priests were either executed outright or sent to the slave labor camps of the Soviet GULAG.

Despite the Soviet Constitution's "guarantee" of freedom of religion, dictator Josef Stalin's Great Terror intensified Lenin's brutal campaign against religion. By the early 1940s, thousands of churches had been destroyed, and Stalin's infamous GULAG had been filled with priests and churchgoers. The oppression of religion, while not as brutal as under Stalin, continued throughout the remainder of the Soviet era in Russia.

Despite all the Communist mythology, the cult of personality of Lenin and Stalin, the constant propaganda, and the falsification of history, the landscape of Russia contains a constant reminder of what really happened there during the Soviet era. The country is dotted with thousands of cemeteries such as this one—places where the innocent victims of a brutal system of oppression and terror lie in silent testimony to Soviet atrocities. They stand as a stark warning from history of what can happen when too much power is concentrated in too few hands. They also call out to mankind: "Please don't ever let this happen again!"

SELECTED BIBLIOGRAPHY

This list is provided for those who wish to learn more about the Soviet Union. These books contain a wealth of historical information and provide readers with a further look at a society that claimed to be a "workers' paradise" in the 1930s and a "bulwark of peace and democracy" in subsequent decades. As British philosopher George Santayana famously noted, "Those who fail to learn from history are doomed to repeat it."

Antonov-Ovseyenko, Anton. *The Time of Stalin: Portrait of a Tyranny.* Translated from the Russian by George Saunders. New York: Harper & Row, 1980.

Applebaum, Anne. *GULAG: A History.* New York: Doubleday, 2003.

Chambers, Whitaker. *Witness.* New York: Random House, 1952.

Conquest, Robert. *The Great Terror: A Reassessment: 40th Anniversary Edition.* New York: Oxford University Press, 2008.

———. *The Harvest of Sorrow: Soviet Collectivization and the Terror-Famine.* New York: Oxford University Press, 1986.

Courtois, Stéphane, Nicolas Werth, Jean-Louis Panné, Andrzej Paczkowski, Karel Bartošek, and Jean-Louis Margolin. *The Black Book of Communism: Crimes, Terror, Repression.* Translated by Jonathan Murphy and Mark Kramer. Consulting Editor Mark Kramer. Cambridge, MA: Harvard University Press, 1999.[1]

---

1. Part I (pp. 1–268) of this book focuses on the Soviet Union.

Haynes, John Earl and Harvey Klehr. *In Denial: Historians, Communism, and Espionage*. San Francisco: Encounter Books 2003.

Julicher, Peter. *"Enemies of the People" Under the Soviets: A History of Repression and Its Consequences*. Jefferson, NC: McFarland, 2015.

Marchenko, Anatoly. *My Testimony*. Translated by Michael Scammell. Hammondsworth, UK: Penguin Books, 1971.

Sgovio, Thomas. *Dear America! The Odyssey of an American Communist Youth Who Miraculously Survived the Harsh Labor Camps of Kolyma*. Kenmore, NY: Partners' Press, 1979.

Skousen, W. Cleon. *The Naked Communist*. 11th ed. Salt Lake City: Ensign Publishing Company, 1962. Reprint, Salt Lake City: Ensign, 1971.

Solzhenitsyn, Aleksandr. *The Gulag Archipelago*. Translated by Thomas Whitney. New York: Harper & Row, 1974.

Tzouliadis, Tim. *The Forsaken: An American Tragedy in Stalin's Russia*. New York: Penguin Press, 2008.

USSR Labor Camps: Hearings before the Subcommittee to Investigate the Administration of the Internal Security Act and Other Internal Security Laws of the Committee on Judiciary, United States Senate, Ninety-Third Congress; Testimony by Avraham Shifrin. Torrance, CA: Diane Books, 1982.

Volkogonov, Dmitri. *Autopsy for an Empire: The Seven Leaders Who Built the Soviet Regime*. Edited and translated by Harold Shukman. New York: Free Press, 1998.

Made in the USA
Monee, IL
30 June 2022

98870628R00105